THE
HOLOCAUST

THE
HOLOCAUST

A History of Courage and Resistance

BEA STADTLER

EDITED BY MORRISON DAVID BIAL

ILLUSTRATED BY DAVID STONE MARTIN

Revised Edition

Behrman House, Inc.
Publishers

*In memory of the six million Jews who
were murdered during the Holocaust*

Copyright © 1973, revised 1974, 1994 by Bea Stadtler
Published by Behrman House, Inc.
11 Edison Place, Springfield, NJ 07081
www.behrmanhouse.com

Library of Congress Cataloging-in-Publication Data

Stadtler, Bea.
The Holocaust: a history of courage and resistance / by Bea Stadtler; edited by
Maron Waxman; illustrated by David Stone Martin.— Rev. ed.
198 pp.
Includes bibliographical references.
ISBN 0–87441–578–0
1. Holocaust. Jewish (1939–1945)—Juvenile literature.
2. World War, 1939–1945—Underground movements, Jewish—Juvenile literature.
3. Jewish religious education—Textbooks for children.
[1. Holocaust, Jewish (1939–1945)   2. World War, 1939–1945—Underground
movements, Jewish.]   I. Waxman, Maron L.   II. Martin, David Stone, ill.
III. Title.
BM105.S69   1995
940.53'18—dc20   94-44070
CIP
AC

Manufactured in the United States of America
BOOK DESIGN AND COMPOSITION BY THE SARABANDE PRESS

Contents

Contents

Acknowledgments

My thanks go, first of all, to Arthur Weyne, and Jerry Barach, editors of the *Cleveland Jewish News*, where most of this material originally appeared. Some of these chapters appeared as articles in other papers as well, including the *Boston Jewish Advocate*, the *Baltimore Jewish Times*, the *Pittsburgh Jewish Chronicle*, the *Kansas City Jewish Chronicle*, the *Philadelphia Jewish Exponent*, the *Jewish Journal* of New York City and the *American Jewish World* of Minneapolis.

I would also like to thank Aaron Intrater, Executive Vice President of the Cleveland Bureau of Jewish Education, and Henry

Acknowledgments

Margolis, Director of the Bureau, as well as Rabbi Marvin Spiegelman, for encouraging me to prepare this work in its original experimental form. To Frank Stern, Administrative Director of the Bureau of Jewish Education in Cleveland, goes a special thanks for his help with many little details that went into the production of this volume. For their support, my gratitude to Dr. Martin Goldstein, President of the Cleveland College of Jewish Studies, and to Sidney Vincent, Executive Director of the Jewish Community Federation.

To my husband, Dr. Oscar Stadtler, and my daughter, Miriam, a special thank you for assistance in undertaking this project and help in completing it.

And, most assuredly, to Seymour Rossel for lending his nice hand and fine judgment in the preparation of the manuscript for publication.

Finally, I would like to thank Rabbi Daniel Jeremy Silver of The Temple in Cleveland, Ohio, for his support and Henry Tyrangiel, former Educational Director of The Temple, who permitted me to devote time to the study of the Holocaust in my religious school class—and to my students for responding so favorably to the experimental volume.

Bea Stadtler

Preface

The events described here should never have happened, and then there would have been no need for such a book. But we cannot run away from ourselves. We must tell the story, the true story. And yet, for our young audiences, present it in a way that they will understand, and thereby understand themselves. This has not been attempted before. Mrs. Bea Stadtler is the first author to do this tremendous service, and one hopes and prays with her that this wonderful little book will become a household item for Jewish youngsters all over the United States.

Preface

Why the Jews? Were not other people killed in that terrible up-heaval called World War II—a war in which more people lost their lives than in any other war in human history until now? True, there were others. Hitler killed four million Soviet prisoners of war (and none of them resisted . . .). Millions of other European civilians died in this war too. But there was only one people that was destined to be destroyed completely because in Nazi eyes they stood for the opposite of what Nazism represented. If Nazism stood for extreme nationalism, dictatorship, racism, inequality and brutality of man to man, denial of the moral values inherited from the great monotheistic religions—then the Jews, apparently, represented the opposite.

Other people in Europe were killed too. They were killed because they resisted the Nazis, or because they happened to be in a place where the Nazi needs were not satisfied, or because of some whim of Nazi brutality. But Jews were killed because they were Jews. They were dispossessed and singled out, humiliated and killed for no other reason than that they were Jews. Even when they did not consider themselves to be Jewish at all, they were defined as Jews by the Nazis. Their beliefs, opinions, attitudes, religion, social life made no difference at all. That is the uniqueness of the story, which is clearly brought out in this volume.

How did other people behave? Did they help the victims? The picture is complicated, and Bea Stadtler tells both sides of the story. And what of the reaction of the victims themselves? Did some of them collapse morally under the pressure? Did they stand the test? What did those do who stood up to the challenge? Finally—can it happen again? Bea Stadtler does not give an answer to the youngsters reading her book. They must find the answer themselves, and perhaps searching for the answer is part of the answer too.

This is an important book. A book with a mission of truth to young people who want to know the truth. It is told with a great love for those who perished and for those who survived. Young Jews may find in it answers to questions about themselves—who they are and where they come from. Surely, they must realize that they, too, are Holocaust survivors. Is it not a mere accident that their immediate ancestors left Europe while other relatives remained behind? Surely it could have been the other way around. Young non-Jews may find in the book both problems and partial answers. Who are these people who suffered so much? Why?

All youngsters who read this book will find in it a story which they must understand and absorb if they wish to understand the world in which we must live. They will, I am sure, be deeply thankful to Bea Stadtler for having written it.

Yehuda Bauer
Professor of Holocaust Studies
Institute of Contemporary Jewry
Hebrew University
Jerusalem, Israel

Introduction

Z*achor* is a Hebrew word meaning "remember." Jews are told to remember—remember the good things that happen to them and the evil things that happen to them. And Jews do remember. Every year on the twenty-seventh day of the Hebrew month Nisan, Jews around the world remember the Holocaust. On Yom Hashoah or Holocaust Day, we remember the six million Jews, including one and a half million children, who were murdered by the Nazis during World War II. *Yahrzeit,* or memorial, candles are lit in synagogues and homes to remember this monstrous deed.

Introduction

The Holocaust is remembered in different ways in towns and cities all over the world. At some colleges, students come to Hillel, the Jewish students' center, to remember by reading the names of Holocaust victims all day long. The next year they continue where they left off, reading more names. Imagine how many years it takes to read six million names.

Some high schools have a week of Holocaust studies with speakers, movies, and discussions. At one Yom Hashoah program, young people—Jewish and non-Jewish—from all the schools in the area walk slowly into the auditorium from the rear carrying lighted *yahrzeit* candles. They place their candles gently on the steps at the front of the auditorium and then slowly walk back. The candles burn until the program is over.

In some synagogues clergy from various faiths participate in readings about the Holocaust during their Sabbath services.

So there are many ways to remember. But just remembering is not enough. We have to know and understand what happened during the Holocaust and how it happened. We can read books, see movies, listen to oral histories of survivors, rescuers, and the soldiers who liberated the death camps. All over the world there are museums that document the Holocaust and memorials which testify to the importance of remembering so that such a horror will not happen again.

The United States Holocaust Memorial Museum opened on April 26, 1993, in Washington, D.C. In its first year a million and a half people visited the museum. Here visitors learn about the dangers of racism and anti-Semitism and the importance of reacting when groups are singled out and being hurt by vicious people.

Introduction

In Miami, Florida, there is a Holocaust Memorial. The central piece of sculpture is an enormous hand reaching into the sky, as though begging for help. Around the arm are figures of people, many people, pleading, weeping, jumping off the arm, or praying. On the grounds of the Memorial are metal figures of children crying and of mothers holding weeping babies. There is a corridor with slots through which the sun can shine. In one area the sunlight makes a yellow star on the ground. On the walls surrounding the Memorial are engraved the names of hundreds of victims who are remembered by those who survived.

The Ghetto Fighters' House in northern Israel has recently added a building called the Children's Memorial Museum. A hall with fifteen stained glass windows of children's art from the Theresienstadt concentration camp houses an art exhibit. What happened to the children who created this art is written there, as well as a description of their lives before the war. Also included in the exhibit are the stories of children who were hidden during the Holocaust and children who succeeded in escaping. The founders of the museum hope that children will realize that the history and lessons of the Holocaust cannot be learned or understood in one lesson but must be studied again and again.

In the Memorial Hall of Yad Vashem in Jerusalem the names of the death camps are etched into the floor and a light burns day and night. Services and prayers for the dead may be held there. The museum houses exhibits and documents and areas for research and study about the Holocaust, as well as a children's memorial. As you walk into this building, it is completely dark. All that can be heard are the names of children being read, children who perished in the Holocaust, and their age and birth-place. Stars and reflections of stars represent the million and a half children who perished in the Holocaust. Outside in the bright Jerusalem sunlight is the Avenue of the Righteous. Trees are planted to honor the memory of the people who saved Jews during the Holocaust. A plaque beneath each tree tells the name of the person and his or her country. *Zachor*—Jews remember those who fought evil and those who caused it.

The Pinkas Synagogue in Prague became a memorial to the 77,297 Jews of Czechoslovakia who perished in the Holocaust. Their names, birthdates, and death dates are inscribed, one by one, on the walls of the sanctuary. In Terezin, or Theresienstadt, the "model" concentration camp located in Czechoslovakia, there is a museum and memorial to the Jewish ghetto. At a Jewish cemetery, where more than 10,000 prisoners were buried, a monument was built to remember those who are buried there, although their names are not known.

In Budapest stands a monument to Raoul Wallenberg, the Swedish diplomat who saved thousands of Hungarian Jews by providing them with safe houses and Swedish passports.

In Poland, at the death camp of Auschwitz-Birkenau, there are monuments and memorials as well as exhibits. Warsaw also has a number of monuments and markers reminding those who pass of the Holocaust. Blocks of black marble and plaques recall events and ghetto heroes. One large monument sculpted by Nathan Rapaport honors the memory of Mordechai Anielewicz, the heroic young fighter, and his comrades in the Warsaw ghet-

Introduction

to. There is also a monument to Dr. Janusz Korczak here, at the place where his Jewish orphanage stood.

Treblinka, in Poland, was the site of one of the most terrible death camps. After several hundred prisoners participated in an uprising there, the Nazis tried to destroy the camp. Now it has been turned into a monument symbolizing a large graveyard. Some 17,000 jagged rocks representing tombstones are arranged around a huge central pillar. Each stone bears the name of a town from which murdered Jews came. Only one stone commemorates a single person—Janusz Korczak.

The Anne Frank House in Amsterdam was founded in 1957. This memorial and educational center was established to preserve the house where the Frank family hid for two years and Anne wrote her memorable diary.

All over the world people are learning about the Holocaust and remembering those terrible days between 1940 and 1945. Let us also learn about it, and remember, so we can tell our children and our grandchildren.

THE
HOLOCAUST

1

Before
the Beginning

You have probably heard about a time, not so long ago, known as "The Holocaust." A holocaust, according to Webster's Dictionary, is "a thorough destruction, especially by fire." In Europe, during this time, there *was* a complete destruction by fire—of Jewish homes, Jewish businesses, Jewish neighborhoods—and Jewish people. This destruction was savagely carried out under the direction of Adolf Hitler, largely during the years from 1939 through 1945. But it began even earlier—in 1933.

On January 30, 1933, Adolf Hitler was appointed chancellor

of Germany and established the Third Reich,* or empire. Ultimately, he became a dictator. During the next twelve years Hitler almost conquered Europe. Twelve years is a moment in recorded history, but so much evil was done during those twelve years that it touched almost everyone in the world, and will continue to cause problems for hundreds of years to come. How did one man, Adolf Hitler, come to have so much power?

Adolf Hitler was born in 1889, in a small town on the Austro-German frontier. He was short and dark, and his family was a mixture of many kinds of people. Originally his family's name was Schicklgruber, but he had grandparents with the name Hitler—or names like Hitler—and in 1876 his father had taken the name Alois Hitler. Despite his dark coloring, Hitler became convinced, as he grew up, that tall, blonde, blue-eyed people from Germany were the most pure-blooded, superior people. He called them Aryans. Yet he looked exactly the opposite.

Adolf was a very poor student—in fact, a high-school dropout. He never blamed himself for his poor grades. Rather he blamed his teachers, calling them "mad," "abnormal," "tyrants," and other names.

After Hitler's father died, his mother found it difficult to make a living for the family. Although Adolf was very close to her, he refused to go to work, preferring instead to daydream about becoming a great artist. At the age of 18, he went to Vienna where he applied for admission to the Vienna Academy of Fine Arts. He

---

*Reich means "state." The First Reich lasted from 962–1220; the Second Reich from 1871–1918.

From Mein Kampf, *Hitler's life and opinions, which he wrote while in prison.* Mein Kampf *became the Nazi handbook.*

Every animal mates only with a member of the same species. The titmouse seeks the titmouse, the finch, the finch, the stork, the stork . . . the wolf, the she-wolf. . . . The fox is always a fox, the goose a goose, the tiger a tiger . . . but you will never find a fox who might show humanitarian tendencies toward geese, as similarly, there is no cat with a friendly feeling toward mice.

was turned down He applied a second time, but the school officials turned him down again, saying perhaps he should try architecture. Although he never followed through with this suggestion, he was interested in architecture all his life.

After the death of his mother, Hitler lived in poorhouses and ate in charity soup kitchens. He seemed unable to concentrate on anything, had no friends, no home, no family, no profession, no sweetheart, and no country. He was so poor that a Jewish secondhand clothes dealer, taking pity, gave him a coat though it was too large for him. With his unshaven face, long matted hair, and oversized overcoat, he looked very strange. As a matter of fact, he later described the Jews, whom he hated so much, as looking the way he himself looked in those days. In Vienna there was a great deal of anti-Jewish literature circulated, and Hitler read it all. He moved to Munich in 1913.

In 1914, at the outbreak of World War I, he enlisted in the German army. He served four years. He became a corporal, was wounded by being gassed, and received the Iron Cross for bravery. In 1918, when Germany was defeated, he felt cheated. He did not understand how the great Aryans could be defeated. The German army slowly dissolved, but some soldiers did not want to leave military service. These were mostly the misfits who could not get along in a peaceful society. One of these soldiers gave a series of lectures and discussions which Hitler attended. During these lectures, Hitler spoke about his own opinions and ideas. These opinions and ideas opposed everybody except pure-blooded Germans and were against every country except Germany. They were full of hate and violence and appealed to the lowest human instincts. The other misfits who attended the lectures and discussions wholeheartedly praised Hitler and his ideas.

In 1919, Hitler became a member of the German Worker's party, a tiny political group numbering seven people including himself. Hitler soon took over the group and sought new members. More people began attending meetings. Hitler found he had a talent—he could "hypnotize" people with his speeches.

In 1920 he changed the name of his party to Nationalist Socialist German Worker's party, the "Nazi" party. He drew up a program of things he wanted to accomplish, again appealing to the lowest element in the country. He promised that when he would head the government, his followers could take from the Jews "wealth" and possessions. To those upset by their country's defeat in the war, he promised to restore Germany's pride and glory. He blamed the defeat of World War I on the Communists and Jews, a trick he would use over and over in the future.

During these years most people thought Hitler was a crackpot. He was the butt of many jokes. At his meetings he had ex-servicemen stationed around the hall to quiet hecklers or to throw them out. Then he organized a bunch of tough, unemployed war veterans. They were dissatisfied bullies who became his strong-arm squads. He outfitted them in brown uniforms, and these roughnecks not only kept order at Hitler's meetings but made it their business to break up meetings of respectable groups. It was the beginning of the victory of might over right.

Hitler's first attempt to gain control of the government ended in disaster. On the night of November 8, 1923, Hitler declared a "national revolution" in Munich. The next day he led his followers on a march to the war ministry. They were met by police, shots were fired, and Hitler fled. For his role in this putsch, this plot to overthrow the government, Hitler was found guilty of high treason and sentenced to five years in jail. He served only a few months. During his time in jail Hitler began to write *Mein Kampf (My Struggle)*, which laid out his plans for the future of Germany and told exactly what he thought about the Jews and other minorities and what he would do to them if he had a chance. Those who read the book said it was the work of an unimportant maniac. Most people paid no attention. However, when Hitler gained power, *Mein Kampf* became a required textbook in all German schools.

When Hitler was released from jail, the Nazi party was in disgrace. Gradually he rebuilt the party, until, in 1928, he had 108,000 dues-paying members. From 1925 to 1929 conditions in Germany were relatively good, and most people did not want an extreme change in the government. Hitler and his ideas about German superiority and revenge for the German defeat in World War I made little headway. But in 1929 a worldwide depression occurred. Jobs were scarce, and food was expensive. People were confused about their futures, and the government was weak. The president, Field Marshal von Hindenburg, was an old man, in his eighties. With his hypnotic voice and simple slogans and promises, Hitler seized this chance to appeal once more to the unemployed and unhappy.

In the 1930 elections, the Nazi party received four times as many votes as in the previous election and won 107 seats in the Reichstag (Parliament). Hitler's emphasis on *Deutschland über alles* (Germany above all else) attracted many Germans. Still Hitler himself was unable to take over the government until after

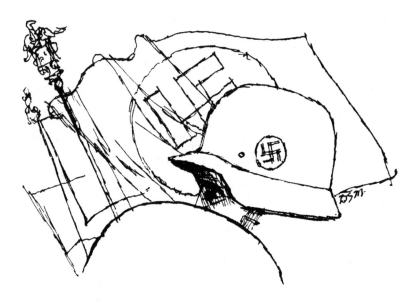

the election of 1932, when the Nazi party had the most seats in the Reichstag. On January 30, 1933, President Hindenburg appointed Hitler chancellor, but he wanted even more power and felt that the German constitution was in his way.

In February 1933, the Parliament building was set ablaze. The Nazis insisted the Communists had set the fire although evidence turned up after the war indicates that the Nazis almost certainly had set the fire themselves. In the confusion following this fire, Hitler managed to convince the Reichstag that the Communists were an immediate threat. President Hindenburg signed a decree for the "protection of the people and the state" that took away all the individual and civil liberties of the population. It gave the Nazis permission to do whatever they wanted. They forced newspaper editors and radio broadcasters to say only what the Nazis wanted said and refused to allow meetings of opposition parties. They could enter homes without search warrants, listen in on telephone conversations (bugging), confiscate property, jewels, money, clothing, furniture, and bank accounts. They could open mail and read telegrams.

In elections on March 5, 1933, the Nazis again won the largest number—44 percent—of the votes. On March 21, 1933, the Third Reich was officially declared, ending the democracy that had ruled Germany since the end of World War I. Hitler was chancellor of the Reich. When General von Hindenburg died in 1934, 90 percent of the people voted to make Hitler chancellor and president of Germany, but he preferred being called *Führer* (leader).

During the next few years, Hitler took control of the press and radio, education and culture. It seemed that all of Germany became nazified. New textbooks were written and a new culture produced. Hitler took over Austria in 1938 without firing a shot, then became "protector" of Czechoslovakia, and finally, on September 1, 1939, attacked Poland with his full military force. This act marked the beginning of World War II. Poland fell in less than a month. Soon after, Germany easily defeated France, Belgium, Denmark, Yugoslavia, the Netherlands, Luxembourg, and Norway. Italy joined the German side, as did Bulgaria, Rumania, and Hungary. By the middle of 1940, much of Europe was under the domination of Nazi Germany and Adolf Hitler.

THINGS TO THINK ABOUT

1. When Hitler committed suicide on April 30, 1945, the only monument he left behind was a country tired of war, its cities bombed and blasted, its farms burned and deserted, its homes and families in ruins, and the name of Germany hated throughout the world. From what you have read in this chapter and from what you already knew about Adolf Hitler, how do you think the German people feel about Hitler now?

2. The Third Reich was an "absolute dictatorship." In a dictatorship, one person or a small group of people rule the entire country. In an absolute dictatorship, one person alone rules the entire country. Hitler had the power to change the law at will or to work outside the law, to arrest whom he pleased, to put anyone to death, to de-

clare war, and to command the armies of Germany. Could any one person ever have so many powers in our country? Could our country ever become an absolute dictatorship?

3. Much of the reason that the Nazi party and Adolf Hitler were successful was due to the fact that they often lied to the people of Germany. When a government lies and deceives us, who is responsible for seeking out the truth?

4. How could Hitler praise those Germans who were tall, blonde, and blue-eyed and hold them up as ideal Germans, when he himself was short, dark-haired, sallow skinned, and dark-eyed? How could the German people believe him when he appeared to be exactly the opposite of those he praised and worshiped?

5. *Mein Kampf*, which Hitler wrote in jail and which was laughed at by most Germans, later became a textbook in German schools when Hitler gained power. What do you think he means by the passage quoted in this chapter? He believed pure Germans should never marry anyone from another nationality, race, or religion. Do you think that is what he meant?

2

Night of the
Broken Glass

From 1933 to 1939, Adolf Hitler, by bluffs, threats, and lies, gained control of Germany and then took over Austria and Czechoslovakia and conquered Poland. This was the beginning of his attempt to conquer the world. At the same time that he was striving to conquer the world, he also wanted to get rid of those people he considered "inferior," of less value than other people. This included several minority groups, although Hitler vented most of his hate and anger against the Jews. He ordered the Aryan Germans not to do business with Jews and placed signs forbidding Jews in their shops and in their businesses. Aryans were not permitted to marry Jews, mingle with Jews, go to Jewish doctors, or live near Jews.

At first Hitler tried to expel the Jews from Germany and any other country he conquered, but that was too difficult—other countries refused to accept them. Then he drew up his "Final Solution." "Final Solution" was a cover-up name for the murder of all the Jews of Europe. Some Germans who were not Jewish opposed these acts. Hitler murdered them, too. He did not kill a hundred Jews, or a thousand, or even a million. He put six million Jews to death. Many Germans had to work on the "solution" to this problem: How to kill all of Europe's Jews.

November 9, 1938, marked the real beginning of tragedy for the Jews. There are Jews still alive who were in Germany at the time. When you mention November 9, 1938, to them, they shudder. On that night all the synagogues in Germany were destroyed. Small and large, elegant and plain, costly and inexpensive, small town shuls and huge city showplaces—all were destroyed. Glass was smashed, buildings burned. Torah scrolls, arks, curtains, prayerbooks were torn and burned. Homes, offices, stores, and any other property belonging to Jews were also destroyed. This night became known as Kristallnacht (Night of Glass), but it was really the Night of the Broken Glass. What excuse did the Nazis use to cause such destruction?

On November 7, 1938, Herschel Grynszpan, a crazed seventeen-year-old Jewish refugee living in Paris, shot and fatally wounded Ernst vom Rath, the third secretary of the German embassy in Paris. Herschel was Polish, but had been raised in Germany. His family had been among thousands of non-German Jews the Germans tried to deport to Poland. Herschel received a card from his father describing the terrible journey and inhuman conditions the family was suffering. The boy felt he had to do something to protest these happenings, so he went to the German embassy, planning to kill the ambassador. Instead he shot the third secretary.

This murder sparked what the German press called a "spontaneous" demonstration. "Spontaneous" means on the spot, unplanned. Joseph Goebbels, the German propaganda minister, claimed the demonstration was a reaction to the murder. Later, however, documents were discovered showing that this spontaneous demonstration on Kristallnacht had been planned to the tiniest detail, weeks in advance, by the Nazis. They were only waiting for some incident to set it off. The murder of vom Rath became that incident.

It was a night of horror throughout Germany. It was as though a single enormous torch suddenly passed over the entire country. The Nazis used kerosene to start the fires and bombs that destroyed the synagogues.

Newspapers in Germany described the fires, but they never mentioned how they came to be lit. The destruction in broken glass alone came to millions of dollars. The Nazis insisted that the destruction had to be paid for by the Jews. After all, the Nazis claimed, the Jews started the trouble.

In Nuremberg, Jewish homes were destroyed with hatchets. Why hatchets? Early on the evening of November 9, there was a rally of about 30,000 Nazis in Nuremberg. A Nazi official made

This teleprinter message is secret:

At very short notice *Aktionen* against Jews, especially against their synagogues, will take place throughout the whole of Germany. They are not to be stopped. . . .

Preparations are to be made for the arrest of about 20,000 to 30,000 Jews in the Reich. Wealthy Jews in particular are to be selected. More detailed instructions will be issued in the course of this night.

a speech which aroused the crowd against the Jews. Then each Nazi was given a hatchet and permission to do whatever he wanted to the Jews. Twelve years later in Nuremberg, Nazi war criminals were put on trial.

Many Germans "got even" with Jews of whom they were jealous or whom they hated or feared. They forced their way into Jewish homes. They beat, killed, and humiliated the people. They stole or destroyed their property. One Jewish woman saw an architect smash the furniture in the home he had built for her twelve years earlier.

Here are remembrances of two people who lived in Germany during Kristallnacht:

Night of the Broken Glass

I lived in Cologne, a city of about 100,000, on a street opposite an Orthodox synagogue, in a two-story apartment house. Next door was our small restaurant. My room was upstairs under the roof and the window faced the synagogue. About four houses away was the 4711 factory—a place that manufactured perfume. I woke up in the middle of the night hearing noises—as though heavy barrels were being rolled about. I climbed out of bed onto the slanted roof and thought I saw people at the factory.

Nazis were going in and out of apartments. Some Nazis rolled heavy kegs from the factory into the synagogue and put it on fire. I ran downstairs and woke my parents. We took a small amount of jewelry and ran back to my room, locked the door, and hid the jewelry on the roof. We heard lots of noise, both in the house and in the restaurant. Finally the Nazis left. We went downstairs. Everything in the apartment and restaurant was smashed to pieces, including my beautiful grand piano. It was overturned and every single string had been cut. Sofas and chairs were upside down and books and valuables had been stolen. My father was taken by two Nazis and put into jail. . . .

Another first-hand report comes from a small town called Kassel. This girl was only fourteen years old on Kristallnacht:

I was visiting my aunt nearby when my father came to get me. He was very upset for he had just seen freight trains packed with Jews. We went to our small home, and about two o'clock in the morning, my uncle from another village knocked on the door. He told us Nazis had come into his village and arrested all the Jewish men. He hid, and later walked 25 kilometres [about 14 miles] to our home. My cousin, who was seventeen years old, had been tied onto a horse and dragged about the village. The two large synagogues in my town were burned. At night I went back to stay with my aunt, because she was alone. She wept all night, and recited the *Shema* over and over. The next morning all the Jewish apartments in my town were ransacked. Featherbeds were torn and feathers scattered. When I returned home, nothing was left but the house. My mother and sister were in jail. Every piece of china had been smashed, every piece of clothing stolen. I thought of my two violins. One was new and the other an older, ¾ child-size. The new one was gone and the ¾ one smashed. I had a mama doll with a china head. The arms, legs, and head were torn off. The furniture had been hacked with saws and axes.

My father was sent to Buchenwald [a concentration camp] for five weeks. We had almost nothing to eat, and no one would sell us anything. My mother had a heart attack and the doctor refused to come. Jewish children were not allowed to go to public schools. At that time Jews could still be ransomed, and we finally were able to ransom my father. When he returned home, he had lost 60 pounds. Later, no one could be ransomed. We were fingerprinted and forced to wear a yellow star on the front and back of our clothing and on armbands. A large *J* was stamped on our passports. . . .

There are hundreds of first-hand accounts from the Night of the Broken Glass. Horrifying as they are, they were only the beginning.

THINGS TO THINK ABOUT

1. On the night of November 9, 1938, almost all the synagogues in Germany were destroyed. The sacred books of Judaism were burned—Torah, Talmud, prayerbooks, and codes. Why did Hitler and the Nazis who helped him to plan the "Final Solution" choose to strike at buildings and books first?

2. Many Jewish homes were robbed, looted, or destroyed; and many Jewish men were hauled to concentration camps during the night and morning of Kristallnacht. Do you think it was possible that the Nazis alone were responsible for such a terrible event?

3. We have heard of people in large apartment buildings watching a person being robbed and murdered in the courtyard and not even calling the police for help. Is this any different from the attitude of Germans who watched their Jewish neighbors being taken away, or beaten, or robbed, without saying a word? Would you be able to sleep through a "Kristallnacht"?

3

The Right to Live

In 1935 the Reichstag passed the Nuremberg Laws, which took away the citizenship of German Jews and turned them into "subjects." A citizen of a country has status, he belongs to the country. But a subject has no rights and is not a particularly welcome person. Certainly a subject has much less value than does a citizen. That was exactly the feeling Hitler wanted the Germans to have about the Jews—that Jews were *Untermenschen* (subhuman).

It was also the feeling he wanted the Jews to have about themselves. The Nuremberg Laws forbade marriages between Jews and Germans. Jews were not allowed to employ German female servants under the age of 45. Jews were not allowed to hold public office, nor were they allowed to hold civil service jobs. If they were journalists or worked at radio stations, they were fired. They were not permitted to teach or to be farmers or to act in the theater. They were thrown out of the stock exchange and were not allowed to practice medicine or law except for other Jews.

Jewish businesses were taken away from their owners by the Nazis and placed in the hands of German "trustees." These included huge department stores and little family shops. If people could not practice their professions or work in stores or own businesses, they could not earn a living.

In addition, signs saying "Jews Not Admitted" were placed on the doors of stores, theaters, parks, and hotels. Jews were not

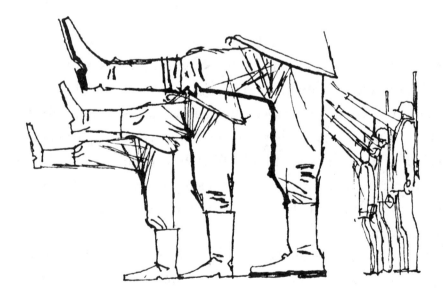

permitted to even walk or ride on certain streets. The name Israel was added to the identity card of each Jewish male, and the name Sarah was added to that of each Jewish female. In school Jewish children were forced to sit apart from the rest of the pupils.

Kristallnacht on November 9, 1938, was the turning point. Before this time Jews were often beaten or forced to clear the streets, but now brutality and public shaming became everyday affairs. Grandfathers had their beards pulled out. Beginning on November 15, 1938, Jewish children were no longer permitted to go to public schools.

By 1939 other laws forbade Jews to leave their houses except for a few hours a day. Jews were forced to deposit all their money in banks. Then laws were enforced that forbade them to take the money out. The money was confiscated by the Nazis. Jews were forced to turn over their radios to Nazi authorities. Telephones were taken away from them. Gradually, everything but the clothes on their backs was taken from them.

Meanwhile many Jewish leaders, liberals, Communists—and anyone else—who annoyed a Nazi were taken to the dread concentration camps, where these unfortunate people were subjected to forced labor and the utmost degradation, starvation, beatings, torture, and, ultimately, systematic murder.

In October 1941 the first transport of Jews left Berlin and was shipped to Lodz in Poland. This was a transport of human beings—Jews who had over the years come to Germany from Poland and were now being sent back. They traveled under terrible conditions, crowded into sealed boxcars or cattle cars,

A police order dated September 1, 1941. The careful description tells us that the Nazis had thought long and hard about what they were doing to the Jews.

Jews who have completed their sixth year of age are forbidden to appear in public without a Jewish star.

The Jewish star consists of a six-pointed star, the size of the palm of a hand, drawn in black on yellow material, with the inscription "Jew" in black. It is to be worn on the left breast of clothing, clearly visible and strongly sewn on.

with no food, water, or toilet facilities. But this was still the beginning.

In order to isolate Jews and keep them more easily under control, the Nazis decided to concentrate them in ghettos, areas designated for Jews and, in most cases, surrounded by walls and locked gates. During 1940 the Nazis established ghettos in several Polish towns and cities. These ghettos were governed within by a Jewish council, usually picked by the Germans. Hunger and disease killed off thousands of people, for when people live together in overcrowded, unsanitary circumstances, disease easily finds victims. In addition Jews in the ghettos were given only about 230 calories a day, compared to 1,500–3,000 that are usually eaten. Many Jews starved, and others were so weak from hunger they could scarcely drag themselves about. There was no fuel for heating, and fur coats had to be turned over to the Nazi authorities. Many Jews in the ghettos froze to death.

Life in the ghetto was dismal except for one thing—the Jews all lived together and most of them tried to help each other to the best of their ability. They produced plays and cultural programs. They organized classes for the children and even had concerts. All these things had to be carried out in secret, because of the strict Nazi rules.

When Jews walked in the streets to try to find food or medicine or to go to work, they were kidnapped by the Nazis for forced labor and never seen again by their families. Frequently, drunken Nazis would come into the ghetto and beat elderly Jews, drag women by the hair, and shoot passersby just for their own amusement. It soon reached the point that people tried to stay in their apartments during the day.

In each country in Europe occupied by the Germans, the Jews were forced to submit to the same laws as those in Germany and Poland.

When the Nazis overran an area their first concern—after setting up their headquarters—was to kill many Jews and organize the rest into work gangs or send them to the death camps. At Babi Yar in Russia 34,000 Jews were shot and dumped into a ravine. The number in other cities and towns may have been smaller, but the procedure was the same: kill, terrorize, use strong Jews to work at slave labor for the Nazi war machine, and send the rest to the death camps.

Many of the death camps had signs on their gates stating *Arbeit macht frei* (work will liberate), but these were cover-ups for the true purpose of the camps. So too the doors to the gas chambers bore the sign "Showers," and the Jews were forced to strip before they entered. The piles of clothing and shoes were, of course, confiscated by the Nazis.

The Nazis, with legendary German thoroughness, kept records of the millions who entered the death camps, and so it is not difficult to prove that at least six million Jews died at their hands.

THINGS TO THINK ABOUT

1. Imagine that you were a Jew living during the rise of Nazi power in Germany. What signs could you have seen of the Holocaust coming? How do you think you would have reacted to the Nuremberg Laws? What freedoms (that you treasure) would you have lost?

2. In what ways do you think the Jews of Germany were helpless to stop the persecution against them? In what ways did they react? Why did most of their German neighbors not help at all? How is fear a weapon?

3. All of us always hope for "better times" when things are bad. In the United States citizens have been in a protected situation for many years because of the country's great military strength. Not since the Civil War has the country felt the destructive force of war in the mainland of the United States.

   How did the great fear of war and its destructive power help Hitler and the Nazis to overrun much of Europe with little resistance? How did it help them in their private war against the Jews? Why do you think Hitler chose the Jews as a special target for destruction? Was Hitler right to believe that none of the other countries in the world cared about what happened to the Jews? Would European countries today care if Israel were threatened with destruction?

4

The Yellow Badge

The Germans did many things to humiliate and shame the Jews and make them feel less than human. One of the things they thought would be very embarrassing was to make the Jews stand out from everyone else. Jews were forced to wear a symbol of their Judaism—a yellow six-pointed star, outlined in black, with *Jude*, the German word for Jew, written in black. In some countries occupied by the Nazis, the Jews had to wear the star on an armband. In other countries the star had to be pinned to the front and back of the outer garment.

Nazi-occupied Poland was the first country to enforce the

wearing of the star. It became a law in November 1939. Those wearing the "Jew badge" could not travel on trains or public vehicles without a permit, nor could they walk on certain streets, or sit in parks. They could be arrested without cause, and sent to hard labor or death. Jews ten years of age and over had to wear the star on the right sleeve of their clothing or overcoats. It was placed on a white armband, not less than four inches wide. The armband had to be provided by the Jews themselves. The star also had to be placed in all Jewish shops, offices, and apartments.

When the German government announced the enforcement of the wearing of the badge in 1941, it said, "Jews who have com-

pleted their sixth year are forbidden to show themselves in public without the Jew-Star. . . . It must be worn visibly and firmly sewed to the left breast of clothing. . . ."

The reaction to this order in Germany was what the Nazis expected. Most people looked away from their Jewish friends and neighbors and behaved as if they did not notice them. Some Germans spat on Jews wearing the stars. Only a few brave people tried to make the Jews feel accepted and smiled or shook hands. One German general was very upset about the badge. He wrote his relatives, ". . . this star is unworthy of a supposedly cultured nation . . . someday we shall pay for it." One wonders what that general thought later when the deportations, murders, and burnings began.

Unfortunately only a few people in each country were upset and dared defy the Nazis. For the most part, people did not care.

Jews who were always observant or Orthodox were forced to wear the badge, and Jews who did not consider themselves to be Jews were sought out by the Nazis and forced to wear the badge. Some startled Christians found they had Jewish blood from some grandfather or grandmother. They also had to wear the star.

In March 1942 the Germans tried to bring the badge to France. The French officials refused to cooperate. They were replaced. But the new officials still hesitated. Finally the decree was enforced in June. The badge had to be worn by all French Jews six and over. Jews had to pay a clothing coupon to purchase it. In France clothing coupons were used during the war for purchasing badly needed clothing. Jews had to purchase the badge instead.

From The Nazi Primer, *a textbook which was written completely from the Nazi point of view. The Nazis wrote new textbooks which changed history and biology, literature, and even mathematics. This was just one way that the Nazis changed schools.*

The Nordic man grows tall and slender. He has, according to our discoveries, limbs which are large in proportion to the body. That suits our sense of beauty . . . the skull of the Nordic man, likewise, grows narrow, long. The face is small . . . the nose is high set . . . the skin is light, rosy-white and delicate . . . the hair is smooth, wavy, thin and fine . . . its color varies from light to golden blond. As to eyes, the Nordic race has light-colored eyes, blue, blue-gray to gray. . . . The Nordic race is uncommonly gifted mentally. It is outstanding for truthfulness and energy.

Some Frenchmen were in sympathy with wearers of the badge, and Nazis complained that Jews proudly wore their badges in cafes and restaurants where German soldiers ate. Some Frenchmen appeared in public wearing yellow handkerchiefs in their breast pockets, and holding yellow stars in their hands. The angry Nazis arrested many of these sympathizers and sent them to concentration camps, forcing them to wear a white armband that said "Jew friend."

The Germans hired several textile firms to prepare 400,000 badges. With the usual systematic German thoroughness, it was decided that each French Jew owned at least three garments as well as an overcoat. However, much to their disappointment, only 83,000 stars were claimed. The rest rotted in warehouses.

A legend grew up that when King Christian of Denmark was approached by the Nazis to force the Jews in Denmark to wear the badge, he said, "The Jews are a part of the Danish nation. We have no Jewish problem in our country. If the Jews are forced to wear the Yellow Star, I and my whole family shall wear it as a Badge of Honor." The legend arose because of the brave resistance of the Danish people against the Nazi deportations of Danish Jews.

Very small groups of people in other countries, too, showed their sympathies at the beginning when the Jews were forced to wear the badge. The Jews wore the badge without shame. In Hungary, Jews put their badges on a week before they were supposed to. When asked why, one girl answered, "We are Jews—why should we be ashamed?"

In 1945, when the Palestinian Jews came across the Alps to try to help the remnant of Jewry in Europe, they wore the Jewish star on their clothing and said: "This was to be a sign of shame; we consider it a badge of honor."

THINGS TO THINK ABOUT

1. The story of the Yellow Badge teaches us that one of the greatest dangers of life in modern times is the danger of "not caring," the danger of *apathy*. Apathy is a lack of emotion or interest, it is being unconcerned about

others. Do you think the German people were more afraid of Hitler or more afraid of "getting involved" or just did not care altogether?

2. In those countries where the people or the government was not apathetic, were the Germans able to force the Jews to wear the badges? Having seen what happened in France—knowing that although many Gentiles became "Jew friends," the Jews were forced to wear the badge anyway—do you think it was of any use to be a "Jew friend"? Is it better not to demonstrate and protest when demonstrating and protesting do no good?

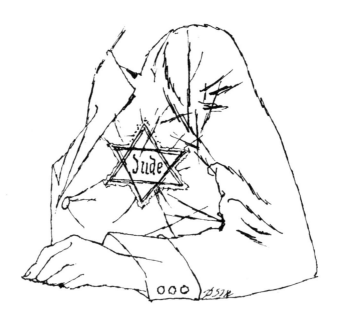

3. When the Palestinian Jews said, "This was to be a sign of shame; we consider it a badge of honor," they were speaking of the same yellow star which Jews in Europe had been forced to wear. Can we really change things by changing the way we think about them? Can a sign of shame really become a "badge of honor"?

5

The Judenrat Government

We all know the saying "Do not judge your neighbor until you have walked in his shoes." Probably as you watch a film or view TV, you think about how you would feel and act if you were the hero or the victim. Would you be brave? Or would you really be a coward? Immediately, of course, you answer—you would be brave. But in the secret hiding place of your heart you are not so sure.

It is not often easy to be brave. Sometimes we are surprised by the criminal, and we don't think of being brave—just give him money and get it over with. Sometimes the crime begins as something very small, and every few days additional elements are added, until it becomes a very large and horrible crime.

In the ghettos the Nazis appointed Jews to be heads of the Jewish council, or *Judenrat* in German. These Jews were placed in the position of choosing who would go to their death and who would remain alive—at least for the moment. It is not easy to be appointed to a position of power and leadership when that power is only for the death of your own people.

In Poland, Adam Czerniakow was appointed head of the Warsaw Jewish council. He had been born in Poland in 1880, into an educated, middle-class family. Although he received a degree in chemical engineering, he did not become successful as an engineer. He did become a successful teacher in a vocational school. In addition to his work, he devoted a great deal of energy to public activities, pioneering in the organization of other vocational schools in leading Jewish centers in Poland.

In 1916 he became chairman of the Central Federation of Jewish Artisans (skilled craftsmen) and fought for the acceptance of Jews into the guilds, workers' groups like labor unions. In 1928 he won an election to the Polish senate but never got to sit in the senate because he was Jewish and so the Polish authorities declared the election invalid.

When the Germans appointed him to head the *kehilla*, or Jewish community, they ordered him to set up a council of 24 elders—the *Judenrat*. Most of the people he appointed tried to get out of serving, but Czerniakow pleaded with them, and finally they accepted positions on the council.

Most people in the ghetto disliked Czerniakow, but when his

diary was found, people began to realize what a great man he really was. He was caught between the Germans' impossible demands and the struggle to ease the terrible restrictions on his people. He was blamed for everything that went wrong in the ghetto.

One day, for no apparent reason, Nazi soldiers broke into his office, beat him, kicked him, threw him down the stairs, and then took him to jail. As he discovered more about the evil intentions of the Nazis, he began carrying poison with him.

Just before he died, he wrote, "Because employees of the *Judenrat* and their families are not being deported yet, I have asked that the craftsmen and garbage collectors also not be deported."

An order establishing the Jewish Councils (the Judenrat*) as a first step in the "final" solution. Reading this order helps us to understand how difficult the situation was for the "elders," the Jewish leaders.*

The first step toward the final goal must bring all the Jews from the countryside into the larger towns. It is to be carried out at all speed. It is absolutely necessary that Jewish communities of less than 500 people are broken up and concentrated in the nearest towns.

JEWISH COUNCIL OF ELDERS

1. A Jewish council of elders is to be set up in every Jewish community. It is to be made fully responsible in the full sense of the word for the exact and prompt carrying out of all past or current orders.
2. In the case of sabotage of such orders, the severest measures are to be announced to the council.
3. The Jewish councils must undertake a count of the Jews and tell us the result without delay.
4. The councils of elders are to be told the dates and time limits, the facilities and finally the routes of the departure. They are then to be made personally responsible for the departure of the Jews from the countryside.

The reason to be given for the concentration of the Jews in the towns is that Jews have been most active in raids and looting activity.

On July 23, 1942, the Nazis came to him to sign the mass deportation order that would send the Jews of the ghetto to their death in the concentration camps. He refused to sign, choosing instead to commit suicide. He left a note for his colleagues which begged them not to think of him as a coward. "I am helpless, my heart breaks from pain and pity. I can no longer stand this."

After his death, one of his severest critics wrote of him:

The first victim of the deportation decree was the president, Adam Czerniakow, who committed suicide by poison in the *Judenrat* building. . . . His end proves that he worked and tried for the good of his people, that he wanted its welfare and continuity, even though not everything done in his name was praiseworthy. . . . The president, who had a spark of purity in his heart, found the only way out worthy of himself—suicide! . . . He did not have a good life, but he had a beautiful death. . . . There are those who earn immortality in a single instant.

Ugo Foa, in the Rome ghetto, kept reassuring the Jews of Rome that they were safe. The Nazis promised protection for the Jews of this ancient city, living in the shadow of the Pope. But the Pope was more concerned with the possibility that the Italians might become Communists than he was about the murder of the Jews. Though Foa was warned about the deportations and gas chambers, he kept telling himself and others that the Jews of the Holy City of Rome would be spared.

Important Jews in the community begged Foa to destroy the lists of the thousands of Jews who lived in Rome. He refused to do so. On a Sabbath day, October 16, 1943, the Nazis, aided by the lists that they had taken from Foa's office, rounded up the Jews of Rome under the window of the Vatican, the headquarters of the Pope, and deported them.

Chaim Rumkowski of the Lodz ghetto was different. It is believed that he sought the leadership of the ghetto so that he would have power and be important. Through this power, he thought he could gain wealth and people would look up to him. But this was at the expense of other Jews in the Lodz ghetto. He was a great organizer, though, and set up workshops, hospitals, and schools. Rumkowski had a sincere liking for little children which, however, did not stop him from leading a group of them to the railroad station to certain death. That day, he said, was the most tragic of his life, but unlike Janusz Korczak, about whom you will soon read, he did not go with the children. He turned them over to their murderers.

Rumkowski became very dramatic, wearing a long cloak and shining boots, carrying a cane, and always insisting that a gray horse draw his carriage. He permitted no opposition and allowed no negative or critical writings. He was considered an evil and terrible dictator by those poor Jews of the ghetto. However his ghetto was the best organized and most productive of all the ghettos. Because of this the Lodz ghetto was the last to be destroyed. The Russian Army was stationed across the Vistula River and remained there for six months. Had they crossed six months earlier to defeat the Nazis, Rumkowski would have been a hero and savior. Instead, when his usefulness to the Nazis was over, he was sent to the gas chamber along with the rest of the Jews of Lodz.

Another leader of a smaller Jewish community was shot because he refused to hand over children, sick, and aged people to the Nazis. "I am no master over human life," he told the Nazis. "I will not give you Jews." In another community the Nazis demanded that both Jews and non-Jews fulfill a quota for a supposed act of sabotage against them. The non-Jews supplied the quota, but the Jewish leader refused, saying "You may take *me* away, but I am not going to deliver innocent people to their death." He was killed. Many leaders resigned and were killed by the Nazis because they refused to be tools in the hands of the killers.

Jacob Gens of the Vilna ghetto said, "I must select people for deportation for gassing. If I refuse I'll be shot. This would be the

43

simplest solution for me. But then what happens? The Nazis have said if I die, they will make the selections. That would mean the rabbis, scholars, poets would go into the oven first. . . . I no longer enjoy being alive. If you know a better way than the one I have found, show it to me, and if you don't, tell me: shall I stay or shall I have myself shot?"

These are a few of the leaders who headed Jewish communities during the Nazi period. Some were strong and some were weak, some were greedy and some longed for power. Probably, each tried to do his best.

THINGS TO THINK ABOUT

1. The Jews who became leaders of the *Judenrat* governments were trapped from the start. They knew the Nazis would kill and replace them if they did not follow orders. At the same time, they felt a need to help the Jewish community. In this chapter you have studied some of their reactions. Suppose you were a leader of a ghetto and just learned the truth about the Nazi orders—that Jews were being sent to their deaths—what would you do? Would you inform the Jewish community?

2. Each leader reacted individually to the problems of deportations and selections. Today the survivors and historians of the Holocaust still argue which of the leaders

were heroes and which of them were cowards. Which of the leaders you studied in this chapter would you consider heroes? Which cowards?

3. Is courage the most important characteristic of a good leader?

6

The Rabbi Leaders

Moses Maimonides, the great medieval Jewish scholar and philosopher, said, "If an enemy should tell the head of a Jewish community, hand over a Jew for us to put to death or all of you will die, the person should not be handed over."

During the Holocaust many community leaders were put into this situation. Some of these community leaders were rabbis. One rabbi said, "If a Jewish community has been condemned to death and there are means of rescuing part of it, the leaders of the community should have the courage to rescue whomever they can." However, other rabbis, when requested to make a selection of those to be sent to their death so the rest of the community could remain alive, abided by the ruling of Maimonides and did not hand over a list. This became an important question for rabbis and community leaders.

During the years the Nazis occupied Europe, millions of people became known by a number instead of a name. Perhaps you have seen people with numbers tattooed on their arms. Perhaps you have wondered what the number meant. These were the numbers the Nazis tattooed into the arms of their prisoners. Each person imprisoned in a concentration camp had a number. Number 187,894 was given to the rabbi, Dr. Leo Baeck, who had been head of the Berlin Jewish community in Germany.

On January 27, 1943, at 5:44 in the morning, German SS soldiers came to Rabbi Baeck's home in Berlin and told him he was being taken to the police station for questioning. Dr. Baeck, who usually arose early in the morning anyway, asked for an hour to put his things in order. Although Nazis usually did not observe the courtesy of informing their prisoners where they were taking them or of giving them time to prepare themselves, they did give Rabbi Baeck the hour he requested. He wrote a letter to his daughter, who was living in London, and made out payments for his gas and electric bills. He was sent to the Theresienstadt concentration camp.

Rabbi Baeck was almost 70 years old when he was sent to Theresienstadt. He was put to work pulling a garbage wagon. He seemed not to mind. This man who had always been a scholar, a teacher, and a rabbi would not let a little thing like pulling a garbage wagon make him bitter. He continued to discuss philosophy and literature with the man hitched next to him as they pulled the garbage.

In Theresienstadt he comforted the sick, attended the dying, and taught the living. Soon after he came to the camp, a Rabbi Beck who was imprisoned there died. Adolf Eichmann, the man who engineered the murder of the 6,000,000 Jews, came to Theresienstadt. There he met Rabbi Baeck. He was very astonished and said, "Herr Baeck, are you still alive? I thought you were dead!"

Rabbi Baeck looked him right in the eye and answered, "You are apparently announcing a future occurrence."

Although Rabbi Baeck realized by 1933 what Adolf Hitler thought about Jews, he felt "as long as there is one Jew left in Germany," he had to remain there. He had been invited to the United States to be a professor at the Hebrew Union College but refused. In 1939 he led a group of children out of Germany to England and could have remained with them there but chose to return to his people in Berlin.

Dr. Baeck knew what was going on in the concentration camps. He spent many sleepless nights trying to decide whether he should tell the Jews what awaited them when they were shipped away. Finally he decided not to. He felt that perhaps some would not be put to death, but rather to hard labor. Why should he cause them the pain of knowing what was to be? It was a difficult decision to make, and it is difficult for us to say whether it was right or wrong.

During this time Dr. Baeck composed a Yom Kippur prayer for his congregation. It was a prayer that spoke of Nazi brutality. He knew that the Nazis had spies in every synagogue and that many Jews had been sent to death camps for lesser reasons, that torture and death awaited those sent to camps. Yet Rabbi Leo Baeck was a man of great courage and strength. His prayer was recited aloud.

At the end of the war, a foreign officer appeared in Theresienstadt and offered to take Dr. Baeck out immediately. The Rabbi refused to be treated as a special case. He had come with the others, and he would leave with the others.

In September 1943, on the eve of Rosh Hashanah, Rabbi Marcus Melchior, the Chief Rabbi of Denmark, was informed that there was going to be a roundup of the Jewish community by the Nazis. When the Jews came to synagogue that evening, Dr. Melchior informed his congregants of the danger and urged them to flee and hide, explaining that High Holiday services would not be held. He made sure those who were in synagogue would inform those who had not come. In Denmark it was a little easier to hide because the non-Jewish community was willing to help the Jews. In most other countries, the non-Jewish community did everything it could to stop Jews from escaping.

In Rome, Chief Rabbi Israel Zolli was afraid of the Nazis. He had heard about what was happening and particularly was afraid of their treatment of rabbis. He pleaded with the head of the Jewish community in Rome, Ugo Foa, to urge the Jews not to assemble for any reason whatsoever. He suggested that they could have services at home, for God is everywhere. He urged Foa to announce that large groups should not congregate in public places. Foa was very angry with the rabbi and scolded him, saying he should give strength and confidence to his people and not

---

A prayer by Dr. Leo Baeck. A man of great courage and a fine leader, Rabbi Baeck stayed with his people, the Jews of Berlin, comforting and teaching them.

At this hour all Israel stands before its God, who judges and pardons. Let us in His presence examine our ways, what we have done and what we have left undone, where we have been and where we have failed to be. Let us openly confess our wrongdoings, declaring, "We have sinned" and in full earnestness of repentance pray, "Forgive us!"

We stand before our God. With that same force with which we have confessed our sins, personal and collective, let us say that the lies uttered against us, the false charges made against our faith and its defenders are hateful. Let us trample these falsehoods beneath our feet. . . .

At this hour all the people of Israel stand before their God. The prayers, the confidence, and the faith that are in us are in all Jews on earth. We gaze on one another in recognition, our eyes lifted up to our God, and we know our eternity.

We are filled with sorrow and pain. Standing in silence before our God, we express what lies on our souls. May this silent prayer go forth and be heard above all other sound.

---

run away himself. Zolli later turned out to be a traitor to the Jewish people, perhaps the only one among thousands of rabbis.

In 1943 a very large transport of Jews was being sent from France to concentration camps. The Chief Rabbi of France, Isaie Schwartz, went to Vichy, then the capital, to protest against this act. The Security Police said it was necessary for the protection of the French Jews to remove those who had come to France from other countries. Rabbi Schwartz argued with the police that the French Jews did not want to be "protected" in such a manner. His argument did not help. Like cattle, the Jews were shipped away.

Rabbi Zvi Koretz was appointed to be head of the Salonika Jewish community in Greece in 1942. He carried out the orders of the Germans to try to convince them that the Jews were loyal and orderly. Many of the survivors of Salonika believe that if Rabbi Koretz had not hurried to carry out German orders, more Greek Jews might have escaped or hidden. On the other hand, the surrounding non-Jewish community in Greece was not friendly to the Jews, so that there would have been little assistance and few places for a Jew to hide.

The Rabbi did try to urge a large segment of Jews to accept work in Greece rather than submit to deportation to Poland, which he suspected meant death. But the Greek Jews had seen how difficult working conditions under the Nazis could be, and most decided to go to Poland.

Rabbis and community leaders were no more or less human than other people. Leading the community meant many fateful decisions. Some rabbis were afraid, some were brave, some made decisions for the community that they thought were best. There were those who collaborated, and those who tried not to collaborate.

THINGS TO THINK ABOUT

1. In this chapter, we have read the stories of several rabbis. Each of them reacted differently to the Nazi threats and commands. Is there a special way rabbis should act in times of crisis? Should we expect all rabbis to think and act alike?

2. One of a rabbi's duties is to help Jews to behave in a Jewish way. Was there a Jewish way to behave at the time of the Nazis? Did the Jewish people ever before in history face a threat like the threat of the Nazis? If you had been a rabbi at that time, where might you have turned for wisdom?

3. In the end, all a real leader can do is to set an example for his followers. In the end, all rabbis showed some concern for their communities, for the Jews who looked to them for leadership. And in the end, Adolf Hitler committed suicide instead of taking the responsibility for having ruined Germany. Hitler deserted and cheated his followers and left them at their enemies' mercy. Are concern and responsibility part of being a leader? Are leaders always brave? Are leaders always right? Do you think that you would make a good leader? Are you careful about the kind of leader that you follow?

7

The Warsaw Ghetto

Warsaw is the capital city of Poland. Before 1940 it had a very large Jewish population. Jews had settled in Warsaw around 1414, even before Columbus discovered America, and some had lived in Poland before the year 1200.

On September 1, 1939, when the Germans under Adolf Hitler attacked Poland, many Jews volunteered to fight in the army with the Poles against the Germans. But the Polish forces were overwhelmed by superior German military equipment and trained soldiers. By September 28, less than a month later, Poland had been overrun by the Nazis.

In 1940 a Jewish ghetto was established in Warsaw, and a brick wall built around it. The wall was to keep the Jews inside the ghetto and all others out. The wall enclosed approximately 840 acres. Since one square mile is 640 acres, 840 acres is about one and a third miles square, or 24 square city blocks. Into this area, where about 160,000 people had lived, between 330,000 and 500,000 Jews were now forced to live.

Jews were forced to leave their homes in other parts of the city and to move into the ghetto. They had no wagons to move furniture and clothing, and so they took only what they could carry

on their backs or in hand-wagons or baby buggies. Often three and four families were forced to live together in one room.

The Germans did not provide enough food for even half the number of people in the ghetto. The bowl of soup that was eaten was sometimes boiled from straw. It was forbidden to bring food into the ghetto, and though some small amounts were smuggled in, many Jews starved to death.

Since the Jews had brought only the clothing they could carry and since the Nazis forced them to give up fur coats and even coats with fur collars, they had little warm clothing. Although

From the notes of Emanuel Ringelblum. Ringelblum was a student of Jewish history. When he found himself trapped in the Warsaw ghetto, he decided to record in his notebooks everything that would help those who survived to understand what really happened in the ghetto.

Another laughable order is about the First Aid car.

The Star of David on the car of the Jewish social self-help, in which the sick are taken to Otwock, is to be considerably enlarged and, what is most important, its color must be yellow—"Jew-yellow."

It won't take long before we are ordered to paint our gates, trams, houses, streets, faces, and perhaps even the sky above us, yellow.

small quantities of coal were smuggled into the ghetto, it was very costly and most Jews could not afford it. Polish winters are long and very cold, and so many Jews froze to death from lack of warm clothing and heat.

Because they were made to live in such crowded conditions, the terrible disease typhoid began to spread. There was little water, and it was not fit for drinking. Sanitary conditions were very poor. Many Jews in the ghetto died from typhoid, and others were sickened through weakness.

Life was bitter. A few Jews took advantage of other Jews and a handful thought they would save their lives by working with the Germans, but most of the Jews behaved in a humane fashion and many even heroically.

Janusz Korczak, the doctor and director of the orphanage in the ghetto; Adam Czerniakow, the leader of the Jewish council; Emanuel Ringelblum, one of the historians of the ghetto who kept a detailed record of life in the Warsaw ghetto—all were special kinds of heroes. All three could have escaped, but they chose to remain with their people and die with them. In addition to Ringelblum's diary, at least two other diaries have been found that relate the happenings and daily life of the ghetto.

Mary Berg, the daughter of an American citizen, was imprisoned in the Warsaw ghetto when she was just 16. She began writing her diary even earlier, when she was 15, during the siege of the city of Warsaw. Her diary ends in March 1944, when she was put on a ship for the United States with her mother and father. In between, because she was an American citizen, Mary was sent to a prison instead of a concentration camp.

Another diary was kept by a man named Chaim A. Kaplan. Chaim Kaplan was a religious Jew and remained so until his death. His diary begins on September 1, 1939, and ends in August 1942. Chaim Kaplan describes the ghetto like this: "If it were said the sun has darkened for us at noon, it would be true. We will rot within the narrow streets and crooked lanes in which tens of thousands of people wander, idle and full of despair. . . . What good will ten decagrams of coarse bread a week do? There is nowhere to earn a penny, and now a loaf of coarse bread costs three zlotys, a kilo of butter 30 zlotys." (A zloty in that time of inflated prices was approximately what a dollar would be to us.)

Emanuel Ringelblum, the historian, speaks in his diary of attempts to grow food for the ghetto. Zionist youth organizations—whose members became the leaders and the majority of the fighters in the uprising—tried to plant vegetables on tiny patches of land. Small gardens were planted on the places where houses had been burned down. Vegetables were grown on balconies and even rooftops.

In spite of all the filth and starvation, some of the leaders tried to raise the low spirits of the inhabitants of the ghetto. Although schools for children were forbidden, they existed underground on all levels. In back rooms, on long benches, near a table, schoolchildren sat and learned. In times of danger the children learned to hide their books under their clothes. There were classes and lectures for adults. There were also lectures and classes for medical students; laboratories were established. Theater groups performed plays in Yiddish right up until the time the ghetto was destroyed. Artists, musicians, and writers in the ghetto were encouraged.

Chaim Kaplan writes, "The idea that all Jews are responsible for each other has stopped being merely a slogan. 'Courtyard committees' have been set up and are taking care of all the residents of the courtyard, even middle-class and wealthy ones. They established food kitchens and a permanent fund for soup kitchens." The ghetto was made up of apartment buildings. Each set of apartments had a courtyard, so many residents used one courtyard. Therefore each group of apartments had its own courtyard committee. Chaim Kaplan ends his paragraph by saying, "When historians come to write the history of the courtyard committees, let them end their chapter with the blessing, 'May the Lord remember them with favor.'"

Kaplan even tells in his diary how Hanukkah was celebrated in 1940. Hanukkah parties were held in every courtyard. "We arranged a celebration in our courtyard for which we charged, and then gave the proceeds toward feeding the poor in our courtyard. There was even a speech full of jokes, scientific and historical talks in Yiddish and Hebrew." He finishes this passage by saying, "At a time like this, there is no better cure than to be a believer in God. Even gentiles are amazed to see our will to live."

Kaplan wrote, "There is even dancing, although the stomach is empty. It is almost a *mitzvah* to dance. The more one dances, the more it is a sign of his belief in the 'eternity of Israel.' Every dance is a protest against our oppressors."

Kaplan felt that the residents of the ghetto tried their best to assist fellow Jews in misfortune. There was a self-aid organization that raised half a million zlotys to support the needy. It was a unity built upon tragedy—this desire and need to help each other.

From time to time thousands of Jews from other communities were forced into the Warsaw ghetto, and the Jews living there had to find room for them and share their meager food supplies with these strangers.

The Nazi idea of having a little fun was to come into the ghetto to beat up old people, shoot children, and help themselves to anything they wanted. But a time came when Germans dared not come within the ghetto walls, except in large groups, armed with machine guns. They learned to fear and respect a small resistance group that organized to fight. The Jewish Fighters' Organization, headed by a young man named Mordechai Anielewicz was responsible for this change.

THINGS TO THINK ABOUT

1. The diaries and notebooks which were found in the area occupied by the Warsaw ghetto after the war was over tell us much about the life inside the ghetto walls. Warsaw held the largest concentration of Jews in Europe. Jews banded close together, forming new organizations to help one another, teaching, studying, working, dancing. What ideas and feelings do you think these people shared which kept them civilized even as the Nazis prepared to destroy them? Why did they continue to prepare for the future, even in the death camps?

2. What part did religion play in keeping up the spirits of the people in the ghetto? Would it have made a difference if the people in the Warsaw ghetto were not all of one religion?

3. Is there any way in which ghettos in modern cities are like the Warsaw ghetto? In what ways do they differ? Is there any lesson that the historians of the Warsaw ghetto taught us that would be useful to people living in ghettos today?

4. Have you ever kept a diary, perhaps on a trip? Do you think diaries are important?

8

The Boy
Who Fought Back

MORDECHAI ANIELEWICZ

On a hill in Israel, at a kibbutz outside Tel Aviv, stands a bronze statue of a tall, proud-looking young man, shirt unbuttoned, chest bare. In one hand he clutches a Molotov cocktail.

This is the statue of Mordechai Anielewicz, and the kibbutz near the statue is named Yad Mordechai. Mordechai Anielewicz taught the world what it means "to die with honor."

When Mordechai was a young boy, it was popular for Polish toughs to attack young Jews—just for fun. Most Jewish youths ran and hid, but not Mordechai. He not only stood up to the bullying Poles but fought back fiercely. When the toughs saw

Mordechai coming, they would detour to stay out of his way. If Mordechai heard shouts for help on the street, he was out in a minute with his youth group to help the victims. He never started a fight, but he never backed down either.

When the Nazis occupied Warsaw and established the ghetto, Mordechai was a young man. He sought ways to help his fellow Jews, and at the end of 1942 he organized a fighting unit. He operated a secret radio station to inform the Jews in the ghetto of what was happening outside. He wrote short, powerful articles in an underground journal called *Against the Stream*. Copies of this journal were found in all corners of the country—far beyond the ghetto walls.

In his youth, as a member of the Zionist youth organization Hashomer Hatzair (The Young Watchman), he became known as "Chaver (friend, comrade) Mordechai." The name stuck to him until he was killed.

Mordechai was convinced that everyone in the ghetto would die at the Nazis' hands. "The question is," he asked, "how shall we die?" And he answered, "We have decided to die in battle." He began organizing all the young and middle-aged people in the ghetto for battle—girls and women, boys and men. He drilled and trained them and obtained weapons, some of which were purchased at enormous cost and smuggled into the ghetto. Grenades were produced by hand, at the rate of about fifty a day.

In January 1943 the Germans rounded up a few hundred Jews for deportation to the death camps. They dragged these unfortunate people to the Umschlagplatz, the roundup place in the ghetto where victims were herded into cattle trains to be taken to the concentration camps. This time, Mordechai entered the crowd with his comrades. At a signal, they attacked the Germans. The captured Jews fled; the Germans scattered in confusion, leaving behind their wounded and dead. The young fighters stood their ground. Mordechai, after using up all his ammunition, attacked one Nazi soldier with his bare fists, taking the German's weapons.

The deportations stopped for three months. The Germans were preparing themselves for a terrible battle. But the ghetto fighters were also preparing themselves. Mordechai worked day and night. He was everywhere. He helped dig bunkers—underground hiding places with ventilator shafts for air—with secret tunnels. There were a number of very large bunkers hidden in the ghetto. Mordechai also helped set up tank-blocks in entrances to buildings. He organized the collection of arms and was in constant contact with comrades on the other side of the ghetto walls. He drew maps of the ghetto with detailed information—every alley and every passageway was marked out for the fighters. To a friend he wrote:

> We don't have a moment's rest. We sleep in our clothes. At every entry to the ghetto we stand on guard day and night. We are making the final preparations. Soon we shall have to separate ourselves from life and go to the place that no one wants to go. But ours is the correct path. We cultivated in our hearts the idea of revolt—this is the path of the Jewish youth—be well, *chaverim*.

*From the last testament of Mordechai Anielewicz. Anielewicz wrote
this letter when he knew that he was about to die. Anielewicz
died when the ghetto was destroyed by the Germans,
but the letter survived.*

It is now clear to me that what took place exceeded all
hopes. In our opposition to the Germans we did more
than our strength allowed—but now our forces are wan-
ing. We are on the brink of being wiped out. We forced the
Germans to retreat twice—but they returned stronger than
ever. . . . I feel that great things are happening and that
this action which we have dared to take is of enormous
value. . . . We need many rifles, hand grenades, machine
guns, and explosives.

I cannot describe the conditions in which the Jews of the
ghetto are now "living." Only a few exceptional individuals
will be able to survive such suffering.

The others will sooner or later die. Their fate is certain,
even though thousands are trying to hide in cracks and
ratholes. It is impossible to light a candle, for lack of air.
Greetings to you who are outside.

Perhaps a miracle will occur and we shall see each other
again one of these days. . . . The last wish of my life has been
fulfilled. Jewish self-defense has become a fact. Jewish resistance and revenge have really happened. I am happy to have
been one of the first Jewish fighters in the ghetto. Where will
rescue come from?

On Sunday, April 18, 1943, the leaders of the central ghetto met with Mordechai as chairman. At the end of the meeting, he distributed weapons and baskets of handmade bombs, known as Molotov cocktails. Some food was distributed and poison for those fighters who might be caught and did not want to be tortured by the Nazis. Houses were barricaded with furniture and sandbags, pillows were placed on windowsills for support and protection. Finally an all-night watch was set up in the ghetto. It was the eve of the first seder of Passover, and Jews from the Aryan side of Warsaw had sneaked into the ghetto to participate in a seder with the other Jews. On Monday, the Nazis attacked. Because they themselves were afraid to face the fire of the Jews, they sent other groups ahead; first the Jewish police and then German and Ukrainian columns. Following these came a squadron of motorcyclists, heavy trucks, infantry, heavy machine guns, ambulances, a field kitchen, field telephones, and 12 panzer (armed) vehicles. On the main streets, they set up tables and benches for headquarters, and they installed telephones on the tables.

Full of confidence in their superior strength and weapons, the German column, singing loudly, reached the corners of the two main streets. Suddenly, a hail of Molotov cocktails sent them fleeing in panic, leaving behind their dead and wounded. One tank after another was hit with well-aimed handmade bombs; the men driving them burned alive inside. Panic broke out among the Germans. The Nazis reported to headquarters, "The Jewish resistance was unexpected, unusually strong, and a great surprise."

On April 23, Mordechai Anielewicz wrote to a friend:

Be well, my friend. Perhaps we shall meet again. The main thing is that the dream of my life came true. I was fortunate enough to witness Jewish defense in the ghetto in all its greatness and glory.

The fighting continued, but lacking arms and ammunition, the Jews grew weaker. On May 8, the Germans found the main bunker at 18 Mila Street where many fighters, including Mordechai Anielewicz, were hiding. The Nazis threw poison gas into the bunker and shot all those who came out. Whether Mordechai was killed by the gas or whether he committed suicide, we shall probably never know.

Most of the fighters were killed, but a few of those who had fought against the Nazis escaped through the sewers and joined some companions in the forests to continue the fight.

The Jews in the ghetto, with their pitiful weapons, held out longer against their Nazi enemies than the Poles had held out when the Germans attacked Poland in September 1939.

THINGS TO THINK ABOUT

1. Mordechai Anielewicz knew that the revolt of the Warsaw ghetto would fail. "The question is how shall we die?" he said. "We have decided to die in battle." Why was fighting so important to Mordechai and his followers? Did they want to die?

2. Others in the ghetto disagreed with Mordechai and his followers. These others felt that help could yet come, that the war might end soon and all would be freed. Some few who did not fight survived even after being sent to concentration camps. Faced with the choice of fighting or following the orders of the Nazis, which choice would you make and why?

3. In truth, we are each responsible for our own decisions. Whenever we are faced by a choice which is important, we must carefully weigh both sides of the choice. Yet much depends on the kind of person that we are at the time the choice is presented. What kind of person was Mordechai Anielewicz? Could he have chosen *not* to fight?

9

A Leader in the Underground

Vilna is a city in Lithuania in which a thriving Jewish community had lived for hundreds of years. There the Vilna Gaon, in the 1700's, had been the foremost rabbi of his generation and created a great yeshiva for Jewish study. Other yeshivot and schools of Jewish scholarship were established there. The Jews called Vilna the Jerusalem of Europe. Even today, when someone says he attended a yeshiva in Vilna, we expect great learning and wisdom from him. Before the Holocaust, Vilna was a flourishing Jewish community with libraries, theaters, and many Zionist youth organizations.

When the Nazis came to Vilna, the first to suffer were the youth who belonged to these organizations. They reacted to the shock of Nazi brutality by organizing themselves into an underground unit. They called themselves the Joint Defense Committee and included representatives from all the youth organizations. Heading this group was a young man—Itzik Wittenberg—who became known as "Leon" to his comrades in the underground.

The young people soon realized the Nazis' evil intent. The Nazis wanted the Jews to slave until the end of their strength and then be killed. What were they to do? They could try to escape and hide from their killers. They could fight underground in the

ghetto or go into the forests near Vilna and fight along with the partisans. Many felt they should not desert their fellow Jews in the ghetto. After several meetings and discussions, they decided to collect guns and ammunition and, at the right moment, to strike at the Nazi troops, blow up the ghetto and the Nazi ammunition dumps, try to flee to the forest with as many fellow Jews as they could, and join the partisans. Although it was difficult to obtain arms, the first gun was smuggled into the ghetto in January 1942, and by the middle of 1943, the Vilna ghetto possessed a number of guns and some other weapons. This was accomplished mainly through the untiring efforts of Wittenberg, who stole through the Nazi lines in disguise. He was brave and

bold, a real threat to the Nazis, who wanted to capture and murder him.

In July 1943 two leaders of the Communist Committee in Vilna were arrested by the Germans. They were tortured, and it is thought that one of them told the Gestapo, the Nazi police, that they were in contact with Wittenberg and the underground movement.

According to one source, the German officer in charge of the Vilna district thought that by catching Wittenberg he would put an end to the activities of the underground. He forced the cooperation of the head of the Jewish council in Vilna and the Jewish police. Together they managed to capture Wittenberg. But his comrades in the underground learned of his capture, attacked the guards who were leading him to prison, and freed Wittenberg.

Jacob Gens, the head of the Jewish council in Vilna, called together the entire ghetto population and told them that Wittenberg was endangering the lives of the people in the ghetto. He told them that the Germans had given an ultimatum: If by six o'-clock the next morning, the ghetto did not hand over the underground hero, the Germans would come with tanks and airplanes and destroy the ghetto and everyone within. Many inhabitants of the ghetto agreed that the life of one man was not worth the destruction of the entire ghetto and asked Wittenberg to give himself up.

The Fighting Force of underground comrades did not think Wittenberg should surrender. The leaders of the Communist group, one faction in the underground, did not want the entire ghetto destroyed because of Wittenberg. The Communist group

*From a Yiddish song. The heroism of Itzik Wittenberg became
a legend, a symbol of all that meant courage.*

Our foe lies there crouching,
Like a beast of the jungle.
My pistol is ready in hand.
Watch out—the Gestapo!
They're leading a captive
At night—our commander in chief!

Then Itzik spoke to us,
His words were like lightning:
"Don't take any risks for my sake,
Your lives are too precious
To give away lightly."
And proudly he goes to his death!

informed the underground leader of its thinking, but Wittenberg did not agree. Wittenberg said, "It has never yet happened that an organization should by its own will surrender its commander. An organization that does this is doomed to failure." He changed his place of hiding.

Finally the leaders of the Fighting Force were forced by the other groups to change their minds. Reluctantly they told him that they agreed with the decision of the Communist group. He still refused to give himself up, saying the ghetto was doomed anyway. The three representatives answered that the ghetto population did not believe that all was lost and was not ready for a struggle as yet.

At last Wittenberg accepted the decision and agreed to surrender but insisted on taking a vial of poison which he hid in his ear. The next day Itzik Wittenberg was dead.

After this the Fighting Force decided to transfer its activities to the forest, and many of them escaped the ghetto to join the partisans. But again the Nazis came to the ghetto and demanded the surrender of the families of all those who had gone to the forest. Once again, the fighters were faced with a moral problem—to escape and fight and have their families killed or to stay and not fight and all be killed sooner or later. Driven to desperation, the Vilna ghetto erupted. They fought the Nazi army with pitiful weapons until they were all slain. It was a situation that was repeated over and over during the Nazi period and a moral problem that became a terrible burden for those who made the decision.

THINGS TO THINK ABOUT

1. The story of "Leon" is much like other stories of the Holocaust. The Nazis often asked the Jewish community to turn over a troublemaker. If not, they threatened, the entire community would suffer. Imagine that you are a part of the Jewish community of Vilna, asked to surrender Wittenberg to the Nazis. Whose decision should it be? Should the community vote? Should it be

the decision of the *Judenrat*? Should it be the decision of Wittenberg?

2. What choices did Jacob Gens have when he was faced with that decision? Should a leader risk the lives of all his followers just to protect one of them?

3. Wittenberg was a leader, too. He said, "It has never yet happened that an organization should by its own will surrender its commander. An organization that does this is doomed to failure." He refused to give himself up at first. Then later he changed his mind. Was he right in the first place or in the last? What caused him to change his mind? Why do you think he committed suicide?

10

Father of Orphans

JANUSZ KORCZAK

Some time ago a Jewish physician who had been in the Warsaw ghetto hospital was asked, "Perhaps you knew Janusz Korczak?"

Softly he answered, "Knew him? Yes, I knew him well. There was only one Janusz Korczak in the whole world—only one man like him."

Janusz Korczak was a pediatrician, a children's doctor. He was also an educator, interested in progressive, modern education. In addition he was a writer of children's stories and the director of an orphanage. Because he cared for each child in the orphanage as his own, he soon began to be called "Father of Orphans."

Henryk Goldszmit was born in the year 1879 into a Jewish home in Warsaw. When he grew up and began writing stories for children, he took the name Janusz Korczak. This had been the name of a make-believe hero in a Polish novel, and this became Henryk Goldszmit's pen name—and the name we know him by today.

Korczak's father was a lawyer, and in the middle-class home in the large Polish city in which he was brought up, the lad scarcely knew he was Jewish. His father died when he was very young; his childhood was lonely. As he grew older, he supported himself by teaching. In visiting the slums of Warsaw, he became interested in how the poor children were living and how they were being educated. In 1903 he graduated from the University of Warsaw and continued his studies in medicine, specializing in pediatrics.

Although he could have been the physician of the richest families in Warsaw, he chose to take care of the children of slum families. He was the doctor who accepted "undesirable" house calls which other young physicians refused. He took time to stay and play with his little patients. He cared for many of these children without a fee, or as he once explained, he took a symbolic kopek, since a "physician who takes no fee does not help the patient."

More and more he became involved in the care and welfare of poor and orphaned children, and finally, in 1911, he gave up his hospital activities and successful private practice to become the head of a large Jewish orphanage in Warsaw. His House of Orphans at 92 Krochmalna Street became famous as one of the first institutions in the world to bring up children in an atmos-

From "Janusz Korczak's Last Walk" by Hanna Morkowicz-Olczakowa. Courage and resistance during the Holocaust took many forms. The "last walk" was a quiet but forceful statement of moral victory.

The day is Wednesday, August 5, 1942, in the morning. The police close off the street. They surround the house. Horrible screams: "All Jews—out!" (in German); and then in Yiddish: "Quickly! Quickly!" The efficient organization for which the orphanage is well known can now be seen in operation. The children, who, surprised in the middle of their breakfast, have their normal day's routine upset at a moment's notice, go down quietly and line up in fives. . . .

Of all the deeds and creations of Janusz Korczak, the artist and reformer; of all [his assistant] Stefa Wilczenska's efforts; of all the games, smiles, and hopes of two hundred boys and girls—this one last walk will be remembered forever: because with one daring leap, it overcame murderous brutality. This small group under the leadership of Korczak has received eternal glory. It is a small group, the members of which are known by name, among the tens of thousands whose names fate caused to be forgotten. . . .

phere of self-respect, affection, and self-expression. Discipline was based on a set of rules adopted by a committee of children selected by children. Duties were assigned by the children, and a children's "court" judged those who broke the rules. The young-

sters even published their own newspaper. With inspiration, insight, and devotion, Korczak and his assistant Stefa Wilczenska showed what could be done under difficult conditions.

Korczak received no salary and lived in a small, poorly furnished attic room which he often shared with a child who had to get away from the others or who needed quiet for a while. He even did some of the lowly tasks like washing dishes or scrubbing the floor.

The six full-length books he wrote for children have become

favorites both in Poland and Israel. In each story, Korczak taught an important principle for good living. Many times he wrote about children who find themselves in positions of responsibility and the things they have to do for the benefit of others.

A children's weekly, which was a supplement to a well-known Polish-Jewish newspaper and which supported the idea of Palestine's becoming a Jewish state, may have had an influence in bringing him back to Judaism. Also many of his students at the orphanage "graduated" and went to Palestine. They corresponded with the doctor. He became interested in that land and traveled twice to Palestine. The second time he spent several weeks with his former students on a kibbutz. The spirit of self-sacrifice, the ideals, and the society built on trust that one person had for another—all this appealed to him.

When the Nazis began pressuring Jews, Korczak became more closely identified with his people. In the fall of 1940, he was told that his orphanage was outside the limits of the ghetto set up by the Nazis. He was ordered to move the children. During the move a sack of potatoes Korczak had obtained with great effort was stolen by the German guards. He went directly to the office of the governor of Warsaw, complaining that those potatoes were for "his children." He was arrested and forced to spend four months in jail. After his release, although his non-Jewish friends begged him to leave the ghetto—and the country—he returned to the children.

On Wednesday morning, September 5, 1942, Janusz Korczak led "his children" from the Jewish orphanage to the Umschlagplatz. Passersby could not believe their eyes. They saw a procession of singing children dressed in their "best" Sabbath clothes, led by a stately old man carrying a sick child.

The scene was described in these words:

> Today Korczak's orphanage was "evacuated." . . . Korczak refused to stay behind. He would not abandon "his" children. He went with them. And so, a long line formed in front of the orphanage . . . a long procession, children small, rather precocious, emaciated, weak, shriveled, and shrunk . . . no one is crying. Their eyes are turned toward the doctor. He is going with them, so what do they have to be afraid of? They are not alone, they are not abandoned.

Although he knew the truth, he told the children that they were going to sunshine and green fields. At the railroad station, one of the guards watched as the children were told to take off their yellow stars and pile them together. "It was like a field of buttercups," said the guard, sadly. From the railroad station, the children and Korczak went to Treblinka and to death in the gas chambers.

THINGS TO THINK ABOUT

1. Resistance comes in many forms. In the Warsaw ghetto, resistance meant fighting the battalion of German armed forces. But the word *resistance* has a special meaning when we recall a man like Janusz Korczak. In what ways do you think Korczak resisted the Nazi terror?

86

2. Was Korczak right in what he said to the children about the future?

3. The Jewish religion has always considered the plight of the orphan a special case. Special laws are indicated in the Bible to provide for the widow and the orphan. What was there about the way in which Korczak treated the orphans which made them love him? Do you think that Janusz Korczak was a good leader of children?

11

The Doctor Warriors

Doctors are generally considered to be unusual people. Part of the 2,000-year-old Hippocratic Oath, taken by medical students receiving their degree, reads: "I swear I will prescribe for the good of my patients according to my ability and judgment and never do harm to anyone. To please no one will I prescribe a deadly drug nor give advice which may cause death. . . ."

The life work of most doctors is to try to heal their patients and ease pain. But during the Holocaust many German doctors did just the opposite. In concentration camps they performed all kinds of cruel medical experiments. Many of the unfortunate people who were "operated" on were Jewish. Instead of using their knowledge to heal, the Nazi doctors destroyed people.

The Jewish doctors in the ghettos, in the camps, and in the forests played an important part in trying to preserve life. The ghettos were overcrowded and had no running water, sanitary facilities, or electricity. Can you imagine how hospitals could function under such conditions?

In the Warsaw ghetto, in 1942, Dr. Israel Milejkowski said to his fellow physicians, "My friends, your fate is the fate of the community. Slavery, starvation, expulsion, hang over all our heads. But in continuing your work you will give one answer to the Nazi murderers . . . and remember, not all of us shall perish."

In the Vilna ghetto doctors worked together to set up hospitals, first aid stations, rooms for child and baby care, and dispensaries. Inoculations were given against the diseases that affect people when they are forced to live together in overcrowded, unhealthy conditions. Disinfecting or sterilizing rooms were set up. Doctors organized public baths and laundries. Their task seemed hopeless, but they kept trying.

Jewish doctors in France organized a secret network for rescuing children, but many of these brave doctors were caught and murdered. In the death camps Jewish doctors tried to hide their profession from the Nazis because they knew the Nazis would force them to do terrible and illegal acts. They preferred to dig ditches and to work in factories and even to starve rather than to admit they were doctors. Some, however, who were well known were forced to serve as doctors. Many of these men and women risked their lives in order to obtain medicine for sick prisoners.

From a study by Dr. Mordecai Lenski. Doctors during the Holocaust worked under terrible conditions. The Nazis supplied them with very little medicine, and the rapid spread of disease supplied them with very little hope. Yet they carried on, against all odds, resisting the Nazis with their knowledge and skills alone.

From a study of disease among Jews in the Warsaw ghetto, it appears that the Nazi authorities were to blame for the unchecked spread of diseases: typhus, tuberculosis, dysentery, and starvation. The Nazis reaped a rich harvest of death among the Jews of Warsaw through the spread of diseases caused by conditions of overcrowding and lack of food in the ghetto. During three years from September 1939 to September 1942, 80,000 persons died of disease, and of these 18,000 died of starvation.

Others sat up all night, trying to prepare substitute remedies from herbs to ease the suffering of the sick people in the camps.

Doctors fled to the forest to fight the Nazis and joined other men and women hidden there. Some helped as physicians and some fought. One of the bravest and best known of these fighter-physicians was Dr. Yehezkiel Atlas. Dr. Atlas was born in Poland in 1910 and received a fine Jewish education and a good general education. But he was not permitted to study medicine in Poland unless he converted to Christianity. This he refused to do, so he left Poland and went to Italy to study. There he received his degree in 1939 and returned to Poland.

In 1942 the ghetto in which Dr. Atlas lived was destroyed by the Nazis. All the Jews of the town, including his mother, father, and sister were taken to the marketplace and shot. Their bodies were dumped into a mass grave.

Because the Germans needed doctors, they saved Atlas, sending him to a Polish village to become the physician there. He tended the peasants with care and kindness. From them he learned that some Russian soldiers and Jews were hidden in the nearby forests. Dr. Atlas was able to contact a small band of these refugees. He brought them food, took care of their wounds, and even obtained ammunition for them.

When the thin, young, handsome doctor realized he could accomplish nothing more in the village, he joined the group in the forest. He became a symbol of heroism to these ragged fighters, who were called partisans. He organized them into several separate units. When the call "Dr. Atlas has come" was heard, there was great excitement, and when he appeared wearing his revolver in his belt, dressed in a peasant shirt and high Russian boots, the partisans would shout for joy.

Dr. Atlas's first objective was to attack the Germans in the town of Dereczyn, where the Nazis had recently murdered hundreds of Jews. Dr. Atlas fought at the head of his platoon, and all the Jewish forest fighters showed great bravery. They drove the Germans out of the town, took possession of it, and on the mass grave of the recently murdered Jews, shot 44 German Nazis.

Atlas led his followers on many dangerous raids, securing food and ammunition, dynamiting bridges and trains. Because they showed so much courage, the group soon began to pose a nasty threat to the Nazis. The Germans decided to launch a fierce counterattack against the partisans. They brought thousands of heavily armed German troops to fight the small remnant of ill-clothed, ill-fed, poorly armed men in the forest. In the battle, Dr. Atlas was mortally wounded. His last words were, "Pay no attention to me. Go on fighting!"

The partisans wept for their fallen leader, but heeding his words they continued fighting until the end of the war.

THINGS TO THINK ABOUT

1. Dr. Atlas faced a moral dilemma. He was a trained doctor, who had pledged himself to save the lives of others. Yet he became a killer, intent on destroying the Nazi troops. Do you think that a doctor should be a peaceful individual no matter what, or do you think that Dr. Atlas was right in becoming a partisan?

2. Dr. Atlas might have argued that by killing the Nazi soldiers, he was doing his part to save lives. Just as a doctor sometimes cuts off a patient's arm or leg to save the patient, the doctor might argue that to save the human race, it was necessary to destroy the Nazi "disease." Is this true?

3. All through the war, in whatever situations and places they found themselves, Jewish doctors and nurses continued to try to help the sick and the dying. Do you think that it made any difference that these doctors and nurses were Jewish? Did it make any difference that their patients were Jewish? How did the behavior of the Jewish doctors differ from that of the Nazi doctors mentioned in the chapter?

12

Women Fighters

Men, women, and children performed many individual and collective acts of resistance during the Nazi occupation of Europe. Each in their own way played a heroic part. But the heroism of the women was especially outstanding. Young girls and women fought with guns and homemade bombs; they sloshed through the filth of the sewers guiding people from the ghettos to the "other side of the wall." They behaved heroically in ghettos, camps, and forests, and when there was no other way, they resisted passively. One Nazi grudgingly reported how courageously an old white-haired woman behaved as she stood beside a death pit, holding a year-old baby in her arms, singing him a song, and tickling him as he gurgled with pleasure. She could have run around, screaming, and tearing her hair, making the child's last moments a horrible nightmare, but she chose to end her life and his with dignity, no matter how much pain she felt in her heart.

Women as well as men were instrumental in making decisions about underground resistance. In the Bialystok ghetto, the records of a meeting show the names Sara, Fanya, Yocheved, Zippora, and Ethel—women whose last names we shall probably never know. All played a part in making the decision that the Bialystok ghetto would resist. When the Germans came, the ghetto fighters, men and women, stood their ground bravely.

Nuta Teitelboim, a young Jewish woman from Warsaw, blonde and blue-eyed, was "wanted" by the Gestapo. She was one of the most fearless fighters in the ghetto and organized a women's detachment in the ghetto. Later she fought heroically in the uprising. Known as "Little Wanda with the Braids," she blew up cafes where German soldiers were drinking, derailed trains, and carried out daring acts of sabotage against the Nazis even in broad daylight.

Dr. Anna Broide Heller gave medical attention to homeless children of the ghetto; food and baths were given to them by other women. Some of them remade their tattered rags so that the children would have clothes just a little longer.

A long list of women who worked on or distributed underground newspapers includes Sonia Madesker, Bela Chazan, Tosia Altman, Feigele Milstein, Rivka Karpinkes, Rushka Zilber. And

there was Frumka Plotnicki, who brought money from Warsaw to Vilna, along with news about the Treblinka death camp. Lisa Magun was active in the Vilna underground and knew many of the underground's secrets. She was caught and tortured but smuggled a message out of prison that the United Partisan Organization should not worry. She would not betray them. She was so beloved the partisans later used "Lisa calls" as their password. Vitka Kempner was sent out on reconnaissance missions and blew up German transports, killing as many as 200 soldiers at one time.

From a report by General Stroop, the German general in charge of murdering the Jews of the Warsaw ghetto, we read:

> During the armed resistance, the women belonging to the battle groups were equipped the same as the men. Not infrequently, these women fired pistols with both hands. It

happened time and again that these women had pistols or hand grenades (Polish "pineapples") concealed in their underclothes—up to the last moment—to use against the men of the SS.

Vladka, a teen-age girl, was able to live outside the ghetto walls because of her non-Jewish appearance. She was given the responsibility of smuggling dynamite into the ghetto, which she hid in greasy packages made to look like butter packets. Vladka was one of the few lucky ones who was not caught.

Zofia Yamaika, an underground leader, escaped to the forest, was caught, and was put on a train to Treblinka. She jumped from the train, pretended she was dead, and finally returned to Warsaw. In Warsaw she worked on an underground paper, was captured again, and was put into a German prison. She was finally allowed to go free and went once more into the forest. Her group was attacked by 300 Germans, and she and two Poles covered the retreat of the Polish partisan unit. Zofia manned the machine gun, and although the three were killed, even Germans praised her bravery.

Jewish women who were imprisoned in labor and death camps also practiced a form of resistance. Many of them observed the holidays the best way they could, lighting Sabbath candles made from a scooped-out potato filled with margarine and a rag wick. *Yahrzeit* candles to commemorate the dead were made the same way. Many of the women gave their lives for *kashrut* (observing the kosher dietary laws), choosing hunger and suffering rather than eat forbidden food. Some refused to work on the Sabbath,

Malka Zdrojewicz's memories were not the exception: women and men resisted the Nazis at every turn. It was not unusual for the Germans to line Jews up before a firing squad, kill some, and lead the rest off to the camps.

In the brush factory there was an organized group of boys and girls. There was an arms cache under my bed as well. Some time later I gave up my work at the brush factory and so did the others. We went to a neutral place in the ghetto area and climbed down into the underground sewers. Through them, we girls used to carry arms into the ghetto, and we hid them in our boots. During the ghetto uprising we hurled Molotov cocktails at the Germans.

The Germans beat us up badly and lined us up to be executed by a firing squad. Suddenly, I felt a heavy blow on my head, and at the same instant I heard shots. Blumka fell dead on the spot. Rachela and I, together with the others, were driven to the Umschlagplatz. They later took us to Maidanek (a concentration camp).

suffering blows and torments because they would not do what they considered a sin.

In one camp women had to prepare an area for the army on Rosh Hashanah. While they dug trenches, they prayed, stationing a guard at the front of each trench to warn them if the labor supervisor should come. On Passover some women ate nothing but a basket of raw carrots or cooked mashed potatoes and one

the female overseer

block even managed to hold a seder which about 300 women attended, singing songs from the Haggadah around an empty table.

Hundreds of women doctors appear on lists of Polish Jews
who were murdered, including Maria Reiter, a pediatrician;
Netty Bahr, an internist; Fryderyka Ameisen-Distler, a dermatol-
ogist; Sara Alterman, a gynecologist; and Rachela Wajsberg, a
general practitioner.

Zivia Lubetkin, one of the few survivors of the Warsaw ghetto uprising, tells of the beginning of the revolt:

> The young men and women who had been waiting for this
> moment for months, the moment when they would shoot
> back at the Germans, were overjoyed. I was standing in an
> attic when I saw thousands of Germans armed with machine
> guns surrounding the ghetto. And we, some twenty young
> men and women, had a revolver, a grenade, and some home-

made bombs that had to be lit with matches. It must have been a strange sight to see us happily standing up against the heavily armed enemy—happy because we knew their end would come. . . .

Hanka was another fighter. She was sent from Lemberg, not yet under Nazi control, to the Warsaw ghetto to warn them of what was coming. She had to swim through an icy lake in order to smuggle herself across the border. When she stepped into the freezing water, she lost her nerve and returned to Lemberg. Two days later she tried again, determined to succeed, and swam the icy water. Then she made her way to Warsaw, to warn the Jews there.

Reyne, who looked typically Polish, was very useful in smuggling arms. The SS man who tried to flirt with her never dreamed she was Jewish, carrying a pistol in her basket of vegetables. Meta also looked Aryan. She secured a job as a typist in Gestapo headquarters in Paris. There she was able to obtain valuable information and the document forms needed by Jews who had to pose as non-Jews.

Lia, a beautiful French woman, was a faithful rescue worker in Vichy, France. She carried funds, documents, or weapons to those who were hidden. She was an excellent bicyclist, and when she carried something particularly dangerous, she would ride swiftly. If she had to pass a policeman, she would let go of the handlebars and skim by, smiling sweetly at him. They never suspected she was a Jewish resistance worker.

Chaika Grossman, another heroine of the Bialystok uprising,

writes: ". . . the true heroes of a nation are small people, almost unknown. . . . I recall the memory of the daughters of Israel who fell heroically on the battlefield—Lonka, Tosia, Frumka, and many others. . . ."

Rushka was one of the forest fighters who often dynamited railroad tracks. One winter day she fell into a pond. When her clothes froze on her, her companions suggested she return to camp. But though she was completely covered with ice, she continued with the rest.

One young woman journeyed from the woods into Vilna seventeen times to find groups of Jews who might still be hiding in the ruins of the ghetto so that they could be led to the forest.

Mala Zimetbaum and Rosa Robota were imprisoned in Auschwitz, one of the worst death camps. Both were involved in underground activities there, and both were caught, tortured, and died, but neither would give any information to their Nazi captors. When Mala was to be executed, she was brought to the center of the camp to serve as an example to others who might try to escape. She hid a razor in the sleeve of her dress, and before the guard could kill her, she cut her wrists. He was angry and shouted, "I will decide who will die and how." She slapped him across the face with her bloody hands and said, "But I will die like a hero, and you will die like a dog."

These were but a few of the Jewish heroines. Some were young girls—many of them in their teens—some were middle-aged women, and some were old, but they felt they had a mission, and they accomplished it, quietly and bravely.

Women Fighters

1. Men and women fighters in the resistance stood side by side on the battlefield. Decisions of whether or not to fight the Germans were made jointly. In all this time the question of whether women had equal rights did not arise. Why?

2. Some jobs were better done by a woman than by a man. From the chapter can you choose those women who served in tasks which a man would find extremely difficult, if not impossible?

3. Some of the kinds of resistance practiced by the women imprisoned in labor and death camps had to do with ritual laws such as lighting Sabbath candles, keeping kosher, and observing the holidays. Judaism teaches us that such laws may be broken if it means saving one's life. Yet these women, who were living in constant fear of death, refused to break the laws. Imagine interviewing one of these women. What reasons would she give for keeping the laws even when Judaism permits her to break them?

13

The
Underground Press

Have you ever really thought about your newspaper? It is delivered each morning to the house. You read it, throw it away, or recycle it. Perhaps you worry about the news, but have you ever wondered how a paper is published? Typesetting equipment, copy paper, dummy sheets, paper cutters, presses, ink, and paper are just a few of the things needed. Someone has to get the news, write copy, edit and correct it, set the type, and run the presses. Needed, above all, is freedom to move about, freedom to receive the latest news, space to set up machinery, freedom to run the presses day or night, and freedom to distribute the finished newspapers.

From the book by Isaac Kowalski A Secret Press in Nazi Europe.
*To print the truth always takes courage, but during the Holocaust,
it could lead to torture and death.*

At one of the meetings of the UPO [United Partisan Organization], I submitted my project to organize a secret press that would print a newspaper for the non-Jewish population . . . after several meetings, I was allowed to go ahead.

The main question was: Where to get type, printing presses, etc. One way was to smuggle into a German print shop and take out what was needed. How could this be done? I decided to call on an old friend, a Lithuanian who headed the German government press, Aushra, to let me work in the plant.

The paper was published in Polish, and we appeared as Polish patriots and told what the Germans were doing to the Polish people, including what was being done to murder Jews. We suggested that it was the Polish patriotic duty to help save Jews and give them protection. Whoever betrayed the Jews to the Gestapo was committing a national betrayal. . . . Our announcements were published over the signature of the Association of Polish Patriots.

Our paper had an influence among the Polish people who felt this friendly attitude to the Jews was the official policy of the Polish underground. They never dreamed the paper came to light because of the initiative of a Jew and that it was published almost entirely by Jews.

When we read the following sentence, we feel it must have been written at a time when there was a great deal of freedom: "Publications have multiplied like mushrooms after the rain." We may guess it was written when competition among newspapers was strong and when many people purchased many different papers. But it is not so. The sentence was written by Emanuel Ringelblum, one of the historians of the Warsaw ghetto during the Nazi occupation, between 1939 and 1944, the year in which he was killed.

How could it be that during the Nazi occupation "publications multiplied like mushrooms after the rain"? Jews were being forced into ghettos, murdered in the streets, transported to death camps. There was little food, no warm clothing, no fuel. Terror was all about—how could the Jews concentrate on newspapers?

In Vilna during the first weeks of the Nazi occupation, there were no newspapers. Then, a German-Polish paper appeared, published by the Polish, full of anti-Semitic articles. It angered the Jews of Vilna. They wanted to publish their own paper, but it was not allowed. They were forced into a ghetto in 1941, where, in January 1942, the United Partisan Organization was established. Isaac Kowalski, a printer and writer, was one of those in the ghetto. He asked the UPO to give him permission to organize a secret press. The organization agreed but did not know where to get all the necessary equipment and supplies. Isaac managed to get a job in a German printing shop, the Aushra Press. At lunchtime, when one of the shop exits was open, Isaac would go to the exit with type in his pockets and lunch box and turn the type over to a friend who always gave him another lunch box exactly like the first. Isaac then would go back into the plant and innocently eat his lunch. Isaac's "outside" man was a Pole by the name of Jan Pzewalski.

In three months, after many narrow escapes, enough type was assembled to start a paper. Now Isaac had type, but where to get a press? Isaac found a small, worn-out handpress in the typesetting room. Within a few days, the press was taken apart and smuggled out of the print shop in pieces. After a day's work at the German press, Isaac stayed up all night preparing the illegal newspaper with Jan and Mrs. Pzewalski. The first edition of the paper, *The Fatherland Front*, made a strong impression on those who read it. The Gestapo tried desperately to find where the paper was being printed and by whom. When the ghetto was destroyed, Isaac Kowalski, together with other Jewish fighters, went to the forest. He brought the press with him and, when the war was over, returned to Vilna, bringing the underground press equipment with him.

Vilna was not the only city where there was an underground press. Bernard Goldstein writes in his Warsaw ghetto memoirs about the illegal press in that city:

> Every Jewish printing plant, including the smallest, had been taken away by the Germans. Our underground press, therefore, consisted of two mimeograph machines, which had been removed from certain offices and hidden. After the small supply of ink, paper, and stencils had been used, we acquired new supplies, but with great difficulty. We worked in constant fear that if copies of our paper fell into the hands

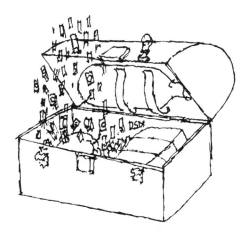

of the Germans, they would be able to track us down through discovering our sources for paper or ink.

For safety the editorial work and the actual printing were separated. One person was the contact between the two. Distribution was also separate from printing. If any distributor fell into Nazi hands, he could not, even if he was tortured, endanger the plant.

Morizi Orzech, one of the heroes of the Warsaw ghetto, returned to Warsaw from a German prison in April 1940. He insisted that we issue a Polish paper to keep the Poles informed of what Jews were thinking, doing, and living through. He was a talented writer and became the principal editor for Jewish and Polish papers and bulletins. He urged us to fight against the Germans for a better world.

One of the Jews in the Warsaw ghetto was sent out to learn what was really happening to Jews after being deported, although it was already suspected that they were being sent to their death. Zalman Freydrich was chosen for this errand. In a town near the village of Treblinka, he learned the truth about the Treblinka camp, the freight and cattle cars packed with Jews, the "showers" that were really gas chambers. Freydrich returned to Warsaw with this information, and based on this, a special edition of *Storm*, one of the underground papers, was issued with a description of what was happening and a warning: "Do not be deceived. . . . You are being taken to death and extermination. . . . Do not give yourselves voluntarily into the hands of your executioners!"

In Warsaw there were three main Jewish political groups. The underground press played an important part in each. The function of the press was to strengthen Jewish resistance and stamina in the face of the terrible persecution. The press also tried to give some hope, that in spite of persecution, they could hold out and would yet live to see their enemies overcome. *The Young Guard* encouraged the youth to continue the fight but not to neglect education. Another youth publication, *Flames*, and *El Al* (Upwards) also urged continuation of study and resistance. *El Al* said: "We have not gone and shall not go willingly to slaughter. . . . Despite the ghetto, despite our misery, we shall raise our heads high and look ahead. . . . In spite of everything our motto remains: Scouts—upwards!"

Against the Stream was a paper for elderly people, issued monthly in Hebrew, Yiddish, and Polish. *The Dawn, Before Spring, The Spark*, and *Ferment* were others. In addition to these, a three-page daily bulletin was issued with news from various fronts. The news came from a radio hidden in the lodgings of Mordechai Anielewicz. *Dror* (Liberty) was an important publication in Yiddish and Polish, and *Bulletin, Our Way, Stamina, The Call of the Youth, Torches*, and *Our Mottos*, were a few of the youth publications. *Shaviv* (Spark), the illegal monthly of one of the youth organizations, was published in Hebrew and *Our Hope* in Yiddish.

Some of these papers were smuggled even into the concentration camps. Many of the "smugglers" were young women who carried illegal publications to far-off places in spite of the risk involved. Editors, printers, and distributors of these illegal papers were mainly leaders and spokesmen of the underground who practiced what they preached.

Between 300 and 500 copies of the various papers were published, and about 20 people read each copy, passing it from one to another. Great care was taken. Still many people connected with the newspapers were arrested and murdered.

The papers told of life in the camps; the reactions of the Jewish masses; reports of sabotage, resistance, and struggle; economic conditions; accounts of bravery; sometimes poetry; and calls for revenge. The readers were alerted to the true nature of the Jewish police, some of whom in normal times had been thieves, smugglers, and the dregs of the community. The editors also wrote against the Jewish councils at times when the councils instituted unfair laws or regulations against the Jews in the ghetto.

One important subject discussed in the underground press was the hope of settling in Eretz Yisrael. "As long as there is an Eretz

Yisrael, the Jewish people will not be exterminated," said *Our Path* in May 1942.

So we see that the written word is of great importance. Those who put the underground press together in each ghetto took great risks. Papers were written and published at the cost of many lives. The people who worked on the press were the quiet heroes. They did not carry guns but used their pens as weapons against the Nazi warlords.

THINGS TO THINK ABOUT

1. Stealing a press one piece at a time, a set of type a few pieces at a time, and paper and ink were only the first problems faced by the Jews who wished to publish underground newspapers. In addition, they had to gather news. From what you have read in this book and what you already know, what kind of news did the Jews in the ghettos need to read? How was the news gathered and by whom?

2. The Gestapo, the Nazi secret police, spent much time and effort in trying to track down the hiding places of presses printing underground newspapers. They worked tirelessly to find the editors and the writers, even to stop Jews from smuggling the papers in and out of the ghetto. Why do you think the Gestapo was so afraid of the little underground newspapers? What makes a newspaper dangerous?

3. In the United States the freedom of the press is guaranteed by law. In the light of what you know about the Holocaust, do you agree with the First Amendment to the Constitution? Do you feel that the freedom of the press is important? Is it better to have a free press or an underground press? To which kind of press do people pay more attention? Which kind is better at reporting the truth?

14

A "Model" Concentration Camp

THERESIENSTADT

As part of the "final solution" to rid Europe of Jews, Adolf Hitler established concentration camps. "Concentration" means bringing together, and in these camps Hitler brought together Jews from all over Europe—rich and poor, sick and well, young and old.

In some of the camps gas chambers were constructed. The German guards would tell the Jewish prisoners they were going to have a shower. They would make the Jews take off all their clothing, shove them into the huge chambers, and lock the doors. Then they turned on the gas and murdered hundreds of people—all at once. Babies, children, old men and women—everyone was gassed. There was no place to bury all these people, so the bodies were burned. In some camps the Germans built crematoriums—ovens where they could burn hundreds of bodies at one time. Auschwitz, Sobibor, Treblinka, and Maidanek were the names of four particularly terrible concentration camps.

Night and day smoke came from the camps with the horrible odor of burning bodies. Yet the people who lived near the camps paid no attention. They lived in neat little white houses, with neat little lawns and blossoming flowers and pretended they could not see, hear, or smell what was happening. They tried not to notice the hundreds of cattle trains filled with thousands of starved, tortured, and smothering people that passed through their towns. They did not notice—or did they?

Another concentration camp was Theresienstadt. The village of Terezin, or Theresienstadt, in Czechoslovakia was chosen by the Nazis as the spot for a special concentration camp. Because Terezin was a fortress town enclosed by a wall, they felt it would be simple to guard. It even had its own built-in isolated stone building that could be used as a prison and its own nearby railway station from which transports of people could be sent to the gas chambers of Auschwitz.

Rumors were spread by the Nazis that Terezin would be an old folks' home, a sort of resort for privileged Jews. The Nazi propaganda was good. Some Jews even paid to be sent to Theresienstadt because they believed the Nazi lies.

Hitler decided that Terezin would become the model camp, the camp he would show to the Red Cross. The surroundings were beautiful. It was built on green meadows, and nearby were fruit trees, tall poplars, and rolling hills which almost looked blue in the distance. Here the Germans took the Red Cross on a tour and said, "See, our prisoners do not have it so bad. Even the food is good; taste it for yourself." The Red Cross, of course, did not know that the food they ate was not the food served to prisoners. The menu of the Jews in Terezin was always the same: bread and unsweetened, black, fake coffee for breakfast; watery soup for lunch; soup and bread for dinner. In fact, a painting called "Hunger" by one of the artists, which showed the Jews looking for food in garbage cans, was cause for all the artists of Terezin to be tortured and beaten and finally murdered. But the Red Cross did not see this. The Nazis showed them how clean Terezin was. They did not show them the filthy barracks with the sick, dying, and dead prisoners. The Nazis cleverly painted the fronts of the buildings and showed the Red Cross a store where prisoners could buy such things as fresh bread and vegetables. It was the first and last time that these foods were in Terezin. It was all phony. The Red Cross did not know that Terezin was the stopping-off place for the Jews who were going to be slaughtered. They did not know that an entire hospital ward of tuberculosis patients had been sent to the gas chambers, so they would not be seen during the Red Cross visit in 1944. The visitors were not shown the storehouses of jewels and goods stolen from Jews who came to Terezin. And, of course, they were not taken to death camps like Auschwitz, Treblinka, and Maidanek where there were gas chambers and crematoriums.

Many artists were shipped to Terezin. For a time they were allowed to work as draftsmen and in similar jobs. But when they

A memory of one of the members of the "Helping Hand." The "model" concentration camp was made up mostly of the very young and the very old. Helping one another was a way of life for those imprisoned in Terezin. The "Helping Hand" was a kind of very serious scouting for the young people, as this document shows.

We gave a lot of thought to how we could not only be of assistance to the old people, but also bring them some joy. We looked through the card index and found out the birthdays of the old people who were alone and on these days the scouts would bring them presents they had made or received themselves—a few flowers, a plaited loaf of bread, or cake they had saved from their rations; they sang songs for them and—in short—arranged a small party. The old people were extremely happy and thankful that someone had paid attention to them. . . .

But we were not satisfied with doing just this. We looked for ways of doing more. We set up dramatic troupes, which on special occasions would put on shows in the grounds of the old and handicapped peoples' houses. . . . Because it was forbidden to pick flowers from the garden, the children would bring them, hidden under their clothes, to the old people. The old people, who were unable to believe that kindness still existed in the world, wept and when we had to leave them we would hear calls from the beds packed close to each other, "Come back again soon."

began sketching what they saw around them, they were beaten and tortured. Most of them were imprisoned and then sent on to be murdered at Auschwitz. However, the pictures that these artists produced survived and tell us better than words how horrible life was in Terezin. The artists fought against the Nazis—not with guns and fists, but rather, like the writers in the underground press, with pen and ink.

The greatest tragedy of Terezin surrounded the children. Thousands of children were brought there. They had been exposed to inhuman experiences in the towns from which they came. They had been expelled from school because they were Jewish; they had the Star of David sewn on their garments. They were not allowed to play in gardens or streets, only in cemeteries. Can you imagine playing in a cemetery? Many had seen their parents murdered and had been beaten themselves.

A few children in this camp lived with their parents, but most were orphans and were housed together in huge barracks, 20 to 30 children in a room. The Jewish officials of Terezin arranged this.

A school was immediately organized, classes being held in the same room where the children slept and ate. There were few books, and teachers were constantly changed, as some were put to death. But most of the children received some education.

The older children, from the age of 14, had to work, sometimes in the fields, building roads, digging ditches, or cleaning barracks. They worked long hours at back-breaking work. But the younger ones secretly studied and drew pictures—on all kinds of scraps of paper.

The children saw bread being carried in funeral carts and humans harnessed to pull them; people murdered; people dying from starvation and illness. They drew these things into their pictures and wrote about them in their poetry. Sometimes they remembered pleasant things from the time before Hitler, and tried to look outside of the camp to the green meadows and hills.

Occasionally the children were allowed to play in the barracks. Sometimes they were permitted a breath of fresh air. But they all seemed to know, even better than their parents, that they had been selected for death, sooner or later. This, too, showed in their drawings and in their poetry.

Sometimes children stayed at Terezin three months, sometimes half a year, and once in a while a little longer if they were lucky. More than 15,000 children stopped off at Terezin for a short time. Of this number only about 150 lived.

All of this seems like something impossible to believe, like a cruel fairy tale about evil witches. Although the ashes of these children have long since become dust in the air around Auschwitz, some of their drawings and poems still exist. Many are in a beautiful book called *I Never Saw Another Butterfly.* Here are two of their poems:

THE BUTTERFLY

The last, the very last,
So richly, brightly, dazzlingly yellow.
    Perhaps if the sun's tears would sing
    against a white stone . . .
Such, such a yellow

Is carried lightly 'way up high.
It went away I'm sure because it wished to
    kiss the world goodbye.
For seven weeks I've lived in here.
Penned up inside this ghetto
But I have found my people here.
The dandelions call to me
And the white chestnut candles in the court.
Only I never saw another butterfly.

That butterfly was the last one.
Butterflies don't live in here,
    in the ghetto.

Pavel Friedman, the author of this poem, was sent to Terezin on April 26, 1942. He died in Auschwitz, on September 29, 1944.

FEAR

Today the ghetto knows a different fear
Close in its grip, death wields an icy scythe.
An evil sickness spreads a terror in its wake,
The victims of its shadow weep and writhe.

Today a father's heartbeat tells his fright
And mothers bend their heads into their hands.
Now children choke and die with typhus here,
A bitter tax is taken from their banks.

My heart still beats inside my breast
While friends depart for other worlds.
Perhaps it's better—who can say?
Than watching this, to die today?

No, no my God, we want to live!
Not watch our numbers melt away.
We want to have a better world,
We want to work—we must not die!

Eva Pickova wrote this poem. She was born May 15, 1929, sent to Terezin April 16, 1942, and murdered in Auschwitz in 1943. She was about 12 years old when she wrote her poem.

These are just two of the poems of children who were taken from their parents, sent to Terezin, and then to Auschwitz to be murdered. These children drew and wrote poetry just like you. They liked pretty things and springtime; they had the same hopes and dreams as you. They played games, sang songs, and danced dances. Maybe, among these lovely children who were put to death—only because they were Jewish—were those who would have conquered disease, written music or poetry, or brought the world closer to peace. Because they died, we are all poorer.

THINGS TO THINK ABOUT

1. Even in the concentration camps, the Jews still continued to struggle for "normal" life. Artists continued to sketch and draw and improve their art. Schools were organized

for the children. Even Judaism was taught. What qualities or feelings do we all have that make us strong when times are hard? What makes us struggle to be "normal"?

2. How do you feel when you read the poem "The Butterfly"? What is there about a butterfly which makes it seem so precious? Is it really a butterfly that Pavel is writing about in the poem?

3. If Hitler truly believed that he was doing the right thing in killing the Jews, why would he set up a "model" concentration camp? If Hitler truly believed the world "did not care" what happened to the Jews, why did he not show the Red Cross the true concentration camps? And why, when the Germans began to lose the war, did they try to cover up the concentration camp murders by hurriedly digging mass graves? Could they truly have believed that murdering human beings was all right as long as they were Jews?

4. Why do you think the Red Cross never asked to see what was going on in the barracks at Terezin?

15

Passover in a Concentration Camp*

In America, we open our Passover Haggadah and begin, "Lo, this is the bread of affliction. . . ." We eat matzo-ball soup, haroset, matzoth, and all the other wonderful foods to celebrate our Festival of Freedom. We may recall the hard tasks that the Jews were forced to perform in the land of Egypt at the time of Moses, but Jews in other times had hard taskmasters too. During the Holocaust, Jews were forced to perform hard labor, get

*Excerpted from *The Yellow Star*, by S. B. Unsdorfer, published by Thomas Yoseloff (with the publisher's permission).

125

along with almost no food or sleep, and live in filthy crowded conditions. The Nazis thought nothing of beating, torturing, and murdering Jews. Nazi guards would take a baby out of its mother's arms, smash the baby's head against a wall—and then go home to play with his own children.

Out of this nightmare came a Haggadah and matzoth. This story is told in the words of one who believed in the sun even when it was not shining, and in God—even when He was silent.

"Knowledge of the approach of Purim and Passover gave us some hope and courage. I approached Schiff, one of the prisoners who worked in the office, and asked him to 'organize' some paper from the office so that I would be able to write a Haggadah for Passover. Schiff gave me some discarded, odd pieces of paper, most of which had drawings of fighter aircraft on the back.

"Each day when I returned to my bunk from a night of work, I spent an hour on my Haggadah. Writing from memory the story of the Exodus of the Jews from Egypt was a worthwhile task. It helped keep my mind off our terrible tragedy and worries about the future. Even during working hours I tried to direct my attention to passages of the Haggadah that required writing. Happy memories were brought back to my mind, of my childhood, and of seder nights at home, when I sat at our table listening excitedly and attentively to Father's recital of the Haggadah which he always did so beautifully and inspiringly.

"Indeed, this work served as a source of great courage and hope for me. It was a reminder that our people have gone through many difficult and tragic experiences in our long history, and have been freed each time, by the will of God, from bondage and slavery. How wise, I thought, of our great rabbis of the past to command that the stories of Passover and Purim be repeated each year, and thus remain alive among the Jewish people. Where would we have gained the courage and strength to survive all our sufferings, were it not for our great and historic past?

"Yes, I felt Passover ought to be celebrated in the camp, and not just by reciting the Haggadah, but also by eating the traditional matzoth. I went to the foreman who worked on the tool bench, a quiet man who had been kind to me in the past. 'Herr Overseer,' I said, 'I want to ask you a very great favor.'

"'What is it?' he looked surprised.

"'Nothing dreadful,' I assured him hastily. 'I want you to please bring me half a pound of plain flour, which I need badly. I beg you.'

"'Flour? What the devil for? Birthday cake?' he smiled sarcastically.

"'For a purely religious purpose,' I explained. 'No one will ever know it came from you. There is no one else I can turn to.'

"He looked cautious. 'Things are hard nowadays, the guards are strict in their inspections, and the atmosphere is tense. I can't promise.'

"What he said was true. Besides the raw material and transportation difficulties, ever-increasing air-raid alarms reduced our working time to a few hours per shift. We knew that within a matter of weeks, or possibly days, great changes would take place. The factory would have to close, and we would either be liberated or transported elsewhere to be killed. At the back of our minds we hoped we would still be at the Nieder-Orschel camp when the first American tank bulldozed its way into the village.

"On Saturday morning, just before Passover, the civilian employees of the camp collected their personal belongings, since they were leaving camp because of lack of work. In the rush, the friendly overseer came to me as I did the final cleaning of my machine.

"He pushed a small bag of flour into my pocket and whispered: 'We shan't be coming here any more. I brought you the flour and good luck.'

"I was pleased. 'If we are to get the matzoth made,' I said to my friend Benzi, who was our leader, 'it must be done this evening immediately after the end of the Sabbath, otherwise we shall have no fire for baking.'

"So at the end of the Sabbath, Grunwald, Fischof, and I sneaked out of the barrack and into the smithy's workshop. Fischof worked desperately at the bellows to liven the dying embers. Grunwald worked hastily on the dough, while I cleaned up a dirty tin plate to serve as a platter.

From Notes from the Warsaw Ghetto *by Emanuel Ringelblum.*
The Jews in the ghetto were disturbed by the lack of matzoth for
Passover. They did not realize how much worse it would be when
they would reach the concentration camps. Yet wherever Jews were
when the holiday of Passover came, they yearned for matzoth,
the symbol of freedom.

April 17, 1941. There were fearful scenes in the office of the refugee organization on the eve of the Passover holiday. A crowd of 7–8,000 refugees gathered, waiting for matzoth and other packages. People applied to receive free packages whose neighbors considered them to be persons of means and who a short time before had been able to help others. The disappointment of those who could not receive packages is indescribable.

"Within half an hour, three tiny round matzoth were taking shape and color, accompanied by our happy murmur that these matzoth were being prepared for the sake of God and His Commandments.

"Nothing was as soothing and satisfying as the knowledge that even in this God-forsaken death camp, where the value of a cigarette was greater than a life—even here, three little matzoth had been baked in preparation of the forthcoming Passover festival.

"There were tears in the eyes of every one of the eighty inmates in Room 10, when after nightfall on Wednesday, March 28, 1945, I opened my little handwritten Haggadah, lifted up the three little matzoth, and recited the first chapter, beginning with

the familiar opening words, 'Lo, this is the bread of affliction which our forefathers ate in the land of Egypt. Let all who are hungry come and eat, let all needy come and feast with us! This year we are here, next year we may be in Jerusalem. This year we are slaves, next year we shall be free men!'

"Everyone came to our table. Rabbi Domany, a little old man from Hungary who lived in the next room, was asked to sit at the head of the table and conduct the seder. I read the passages from the Haggadah as loudly as I dared, and the rest followed in a whisper. Then, raising the rusty cup of black coffee which he had saved from the morning in place of the traditional cup of red wine, Rabbi Domany called out in a tear-choked voice the words of the Haggadah:

And it is this promise which has stood by our ancestors and by us. For it was not just one person who rose up against us to destroy us, but in every generation men rise against us. But the Holy One, blessed be He, delivers us from their hand.

"How true were the words that evening. Never before have so many men at one and the same time been so overawed in their trust of Almighty God as on that evening in Room 10 at Nieder-Orschel; never before was there such a truly solemn seder service; never before was there such longing for God and His protective arm."

THINGS TO THINK ABOUT

1. When all books had been taken away, S. B. Unsdorfer was still able to "write" a Haggadah. If all books were taken from you, what stories would you be able to write from memory? If you could have only two sheets of paper, which story would you write down to share with your friends? Why would you choose that story above all the rest? Why did Unsdorfer choose the Haggadah?

2. Reading the story of the baking of the matzoth might remind you of how the presses were built for the underground newspapers. Do you think the baking of the matzoth was a kind of resistance? Was the Passover seder a kind of resistance?

3. What special meaning did the holiday of Passover hold for these imprisoned Jews? Why do you think that they had not lost their faith?

16

Danish Rescue

The Germans met very little resistance in their occupation of European countries. But two tiny countries, the Netherlands and Denmark, caused the Germans the most trouble. Denmark's resistance was unique and especially effective. The Danes protected, hid, and saved 98.5 percent of their Jewish population, which numbered 8,000.

One of the most effective underground groups involved in anti-Nazi activities and in saving Jews was located in the town of Elsinore. Danes from all walks of life participated in this underground ring, which called itself the Elsinore Sewing Club. Borge

Ronne, a newspaper correspondent; Erlin Kiaer, a bookbinder; Thomond Larsen, a detective; Ove Bruhn, a bookkeeper; and Jorgens Gersfelt, a physician, gathered together as the center of the underground. Like most Danes they were disturbed when Denmark gave in to Germany in 1940 without firing one shot. But in 1943, when the Germans decided to round up all Denmark's Jews and send them to death camps, the Danes cooperated to save their Jewish neighbors. Danes disliked the Germans from previous encounters with them. Also, they did not regard Jews as separate people, but rather as Danes. It was not a written or voted decision. It was just something that happened.

An entire Danish uprising began the morning of Friday, September 30, 1943. It was the day before Rosh Hashanah, and Rabbi Marcus Melchior, Chief Rabbi of Denmark, stood before about 150 members of his synagogue in Copenhagen. He warned them that he had word that on the next day the Germans were planning to raid all Jewish homes and ship the Jews to concentration camps. He urged those present to contact everyone they knew who was Jewish and to contact Christian friends and urge them to report the dreadful news to their Jewish friends. This had to be done immediately, so that by night all the Jews would be in hiding.

Rabbi Melchior was married and had five children. No one person could hide such a large family, so the Rabbi decided they would have to separate. He was also worried about where to hide the precious ritual objects such as the Torah scrolls and the prayerbooks. He called on his friend, Pastor Hans Kildeby, who lived 60 miles south of Copenhagen. The Pastor insisted the

Proclamation of the Danish Freedom Council. Early on, the Danish people realized that a threat to the freedom of the Jews was a threat to the freedom of all Denmark. In this brave northern country, resistance became an everyday way of life during the Nazi occupation.

The Danish Freedom Council condemns the pogroms the Germans have set in motion against the Jews in our country. Among the Danish people the Jews are not a special class but are citizens to exactly the same degree as all other Danes. . . . We Danes know that the whole population stands behind resistance to the German oppressors. The Council calls on the Danish population to help in every way possible those Jewish fellow-citizens who have not yet succeeded in escaping abroad. Every Dane who renders help to the Germans in their persecution of human beings is a traitor and will be punished as such when Germany is defeated.

whole family come to him. Then Melchior contacted another Lutheran minister in Copenhagen, who agreed to hide the ritual objects in the basement of his church.

Much of the Danish behavior was spontaneous. On the day of the secret announcement, a young ambulance driver was told of the trouble. He took a phone book, circled all the Jewish names, and drove through the entire city warning these people. When some became frantic, not knowing where they could hide, he put them into his ambulance and drove them to Bispebjerg Hospital, where he knew Dr. Karl Køster would hide them. When questioned why he had done this, he said, "What else could I do?"

Professor Richard Ege, later a biochemist at the Rockefeller Institute, when asked why he had hidden so many Jews in his building, said, "It was a natural reaction to want to help good friends." And his wife said, "It was exactly the same as seeing a neighbor's house on fire. Naturally you want to do something about it." One pastor said, "I would rather die with the Jews than live with the Nazis."

The Jews could not hide forever. But where could they go? Neutral Sweden seemed to be the logical place for them, but would Sweden agree? Who could convince the authorities in that country? The Nobel Prize winner Niels Bohr was one of the two most famous nuclear physicists in the world (Albert Einstein was the other). On September 30 he was smuggled out of Denmark into Sweden. Upon arrival Bohr was told he would have to go to London to be safe from the Nazis. He refused.

He would not leave Sweden, Bohr said, until he could speak with the Swedish foreign minister. In Stockholm he told the foreign minister he could not leave until Sweden opened its doors for the Jewish refugees. The minister was uncooperative. Bohr became angry and insisted on seeing King Gustav. After meeting with the King, he was assured that Sweden would accept the Jews. Bohr then asked that Sweden announce its decision on the front pages of its newspapers and in a radio broadcast to Denmark. After the broadcast, Bohr left for England and from there went to the United States.

Because Elsinore was separated from Sweden by a waterway

only two and one-half miles wide, it was the best place for the refugees to cross. Mostly the Elsinore Sewing Club used fishing boats, even purchasing two boats for this purpose. Each man in the group had a special job. When children were hidden or taken on boats, Dr. Gersfelt was charged with keeping the younger ones quiet. Sleeping pills wore off too soon. So although he was afraid of injecting narcotics (not knowing the exact amounts he should use and what would be the effect on the children), he was forced to do so in order to get the children past the German checkpoints. He waited anxiously for news of the first transport to Sweden, to hear how the injected children had fared. When he found they arrived in good health, he injected others without hesitation. As a physician, he also had an extra gas ration and was able to serve as a driver. Kiaer manned the boats and took so many Jews over he became known as the "Danish Pimpernel," and was hunted by the Nazis. Finally captured and tortured, he never revealed any information.

Mogens Staffeldt owned a bookstore. The Nazis took over the entire building in which the bookstore was housed. Mr. Staffeldt moved across the street. Here another very active underground group met, and it was decided that the empty back room would be used as a collection point for refugees before taking them to the boats. If a certain book of poems was in the window, it meant the coast was clear for the refugees. However, if the book was absent, it meant that Jews should not enter.

The men in the underground praised the Jews. "They were very frightened," they said, "but courageous and often noble. If there was not enough room in a boat, there was trouble—not because each wanted to go, but because each adult male insisted on staying behind. One elderly Jew said, 'I'm seventy. Why should I go? Maybe I'll die next year. This man is forty—let him go.'" About 600 Jews were saved through the efforts of the bookstore group.

King Christian X, Denmark's leader, was the most important symbol of Denmark's spirit of defiance against the Nazis. He was a good and reliable friend to the Jews. Throughout the occupation of Denmark by the Germans, he refused to turn over any Jew for deportation.

One of the Danish rescuers described his homeland as "a little nation without much ambition, even a feeling of inferiority, but Danes can be tough, brave, and resistant to what they feel is injustice." General Dwight Eisenhower, head of the Allied armed forces during World War II, said, "The Danish people surprised the world with resistance second to none."

The people of Denmark sacrificed themselves in order to save fellow human beings from death. If you ever hear the Danish national anthem beginning with the words "It is a lovely land," you can believe it.

THINGS TO THINK ABOUT

1. In 1943 when the Germans prepared to round up Jews living in Denmark, the Danish people united to save their Jewish neighbors. The great majority of the nation banded together in this effort. From what you know of history in general and of Jewish history—consider the

governments, religious beliefs, and ways of life—why do you think the Danish people acted differently from the Polish people or the people of Russia?

2. Germany was not the only nation which set up concentration camps. During World War II, the United States and Canada established concentration camps for some of their own citizens of Japanese ancestry. And the British established concentration camps for Jews who were caught trying to enter Palestine illegally. Of course, there were differences between these concentration camps and those of the Nazis. What were the differences? Do you think that living in a country of freedom like the United States or Britain should give us a respect for the freedoms of other people? (If you do not know about the concentration camps in the United States and Canada during World War II, ask your teacher to help you locate information.)

3. After leaving Sweden, Niels Bohr made his way to the United States. He worked in Los Alamos, New Mexico, helping the United States develop the atomic bomb. In 1945, when the war was over, Bohr returned to Copenhagen to take up his position as a college professor. Was Bohr wrong when he demanded that the king of Sweden protect the Jewish people? Was Bohr wrong in helping with the design of the atomic bomb? What events made it possible for Niels Bohr to have done two things so opposite from one another?

17

The Righteous Gentiles

Yad Vashem, the Holocaust Memorial in Jerusalem, is located on the Mount of Remembrance. The road leading to the building is called the Avenue of the Righteous. It is lined with trees planted to honor righteous Gentiles, or non-Jews, who helped save Jews during the Holocaust. Each tree bears a plaque telling about the person in whose memory or honor the tree is planted and the words "He who saves a single life, it is as though he has saved the entire world."

One tree is planted in memory of a Dutch citizen—Joop Westerwill, a courageous and noble man who helped hundreds of Jewish children and teenagers escape the Nazis.

The Dutch people strongly believe in justice, decency, and freedom. To Joop these values meant more than life itself. A teacher and principal of a school in Rotterdam when Germany invaded the Netherlands, Joop was approached by some young Jews asking him to help hide and assist in the escape of Jewish children. "I have been waiting and hoping for this," he said. "When one tries to teach in the face of this humiliation to humanity, it is impossible."

Joop rented apartments in his own name and let Jewish families live in them. At times he had three apartments filled with Jews trying to escape deportation. Once he wrote he would have liked to be Jewish. "You Jews are unique and have the highest regard for human values. In the face of the persecution and shame the Nazis heap upon you, you still hold your heads high and instill culture in yourselves and your children." Joop always encouraged Jewish children in hiding to continue their studies and often said that after Germany was defeated, he, his wife, and four children would go to Palestine and settle on a kibbutz.

On one trip in 1944 he took a group of children to the Spanish border. The children were tired, frightened, dirty, and cold. Before he left them, he spoke to them in words they remembered many years later. One child who survived, Sophia Nussbaum, said, "I'll never forget him. In those dark days he was the only spark of humanity."

For twenty months Joop did his lifesaving work, sometimes sleeping only two hours a night, because by day he continued to work as principal of the school. On March 11, 1944, Joop was captured by the Nazis while trying to smuggle two girls into France. In jail he was constantly beaten and tortured but would give no information. When in solitary confinement he taught songs and gave lectures to others in nearby cells. In August 1944 he was shot by the Nazis, although his friends had tried to arrange his release.

Oskar Schindler, a German Catholic industrialist, had an enamelware factory in Cracow, Poland. He employed several hundred Jews whom he saved by bribing German officials who wanted to deport them to death camps. He managed to find food for "his Jews" and kept them in the factory. When the factory moved to Czechoslovakia, he brought his Jews with him. In the new location they made punch presses and then shells for guns. Schindler told the Germans he needed these people, even children, for the war effort and somehow saved them all.

Schindler was determined to keep "his Jews" and even went to the death camp Auschwitz once to rescue some of his Jewish women and children who had been sent there by mistake. Although food was scarce, he did everything possible to feed "his

Jews" and provide them with a safe place to live. After the war he moved to South America and became quite poor. But he was always helped by his grateful Jews all over the world, and when he died, he was buried in a Christian cemetery in Jerusalem.

Every person who helped hide and keep Jews put his or her life in danger. Nevertheless, the list of righteous Gentiles is a long one. Staszek Jackowski, a young Catholic carriage maker, lived in the Polish town of Stanislaw. As a young boy, he had a Jewish friend, Max Saginur. When the Nazis sent the Jews from the nearby ghetto to concentration camps, Staszek found his friend Max and brought him home. As the war continued, he hid thirty-one other Jews in a bunker underneath his house. Toward the end of the war he told Max, "I never thought there would be thirty-two of you. I did it for you. I know you would do the same for me. If they catch me saving you, they will kill me. I might as well be killed for saving thirty-two as for one." But he was not killed. Some of the Jews he saved later brought him and his family to New York and supported him until he found work.

Hans Fritz Graebe, a German engineer, saved the lives of hundreds of Jews by employing them on engineering jobs, often at his own expense. Fritz was stationed near the Russian border, where mobile killing units rounded up Jews and shot them so they fell into a pit. Fritz was sickened by the sight. He thought about his mother's question when something evil happened— "Fritz, what would you do?" It was his mother's sense of justice that she had instilled in him at an early age that caused him to act in this heroic way. Although he was questioned several times by the Nazis, he continued with his difficult, brave work.

Aristedes De Sousa Mendes, the Portuguese consul in Bordeaux, France, during the war, wrote thousands of visas for Jews to go to Portugal through Spain. Spain and Portugal were neutral countries in the war, and the Portuguese authorities forbade him to do this, but he continued until he was physically brought back to Portugal. All his property and wealth were taken away, and he was not allowed to practice law any more. His family, including his wife and fourteen children, was very poor, but he said, "I had to save these people—as many as I could. If I was disobeying orders, I would rather be with God against men than with men against God."

Raoul Wallenberg was a Swedish diplomat who was responsible for saving thousands of Hungarian Jews from death. He established "safe houses" in Budapest which he purchased or rented and from which he flew the Swedish flag. He issued Swedish passports to 20,000 Jews and created special shelters which housed 8,000 children. One woman he saved said, "He gave us a sense that we were still human beings," something the Nazis had taken away from them. When Wallenberg learned that the Germans planned to destroy the Jewish ghetto, with its 70,000 Jews, he threatened the German commander that he would see him hanged for war crimes if he went ahead with the slaughter. It was near the end of the war, and the Nazi backed down. In an indirect way, Wallenberg had saved another 70,000 Jews. In all Wallenberg saved about 100,000 Jews from certain death.

The people of LeChambon, France, a village in the mountains of southern France, managed to save about 5,000 Jews. Pastor Andre Trocme, the minister of the village, and his wife, Magda, were Protestants. They protested the treatment of the Jews. The youth of LeChambon wrote a letter to the minister of youth in Vichy, the Nazi headquarters in France, and said, yes, there were Jews in LeChambon, but since there was no difference between Jews and non-Jews, LeChambon would disobey any orders to deport them. A couple of weeks later, a high official of the Vichy government came to LeChambon and demanded the names and addresses of Jews hidden there. Since all the Jews had false identity cards, Trocme told the truth when he said he did not know their names.

The pastor's house was a stopping-off place for refugees who passed through the town. As soon as possible, they were moved to a more permanent shelter. Then a team of men took them across the mountains to Switzerland, which was a neutral country.

Trocme was arrested with two other men from LeChambon. They were released about a month later. When refugees knocked on the door of Magda and Andre Trocme's home, Magda would say, "Naturally come in, yes, come in."

Sometimes goodness was in one person, sometimes in a group of people, occasionally in an entire village, once in an entire country—Denmark. The world must be grateful for these courageous human beings who knew they could be killed for what they did but did it in spite of personal danger.

THINGS TO THINK ABOUT

1. Joop Westerwill tried to help his Jewish children continue with their Jewish studies. Sometimes when children

were left with Catholic nuns or priests, they would convert the Jewish child to Christianity. Joop had a deep respect for the religion of the Jewish children he helped. Can we respect another person's beliefs without wanting to change them? How could the Catholics explain their actions? How could Joop Westerwill explain his actions?

2. To help Jews, Joop gave up everything he had. From what you read of his life, what ideals did he have that made him a good teacher? Did he ever really stop teaching?

3. What incidents show that Jews never forget those who have been kind to them and helped them when they were in danger or need?

4. What did Staszek Jackowski tell his Jewish friend? Was he right?

5. What was one of the reasons Hans Fritz Graebe helped save Jews?

6. Was Aristedes De Sousa Mendes a brave man? Was he fighting the system? What did he say? Was he right?

7. Why did Jews want to work for Oskar Schindler?

8. One woman saved by Raoul Wallenberg said, "He gave us a sense that we were still human beings." What did she mean by that?

9. There was not one person in LeChambon who collaborated or helped the Nazis find the Jews hidden there. Why?

10. Do you think you could have, and would have, acted as bravely as these righteous people under these circumstances?

18

The Lady with the Stamps

The word "propaganda" means an organized effort to spread particular ideas or beliefs to advance a cause. When used in politics, propaganda often presents only half the truth. A group or government may tell only those facts which make its side seem completely right and its enemies completely wrong. At its worst, propaganda can be the spreading of ugly lies to stir up hatred against a particular group of people.

This is the kind of propaganda the Nazis used against the Jews. They tried to represent the Jews as subhuman so that non-

---

*A personal statement by Irene Harand. Mrs. Harand's stamp
campaign made her the sworn enemy of the Nazi party. In her
quiet way she helped to force truth to shine in the darkest
corners of Nazi-controlled Europe.*

Today is the 25th anniversary of the unbelievably inhumane
day of November 10, 1938 (Kristallnacht*), when Hitler's
hordes in Germany began the rounding up of thousands and
thousands of perfectly innocent and decent human beings to
throw them into concentration camps. The only "crime" of
these people was that they were born Jews . . . and the whole
world looked on . . . I, myself, was only carrying the flag.
Without my followers none would have noticed.

*Kristallnacht occurred in Austria, too, where it is commemorated on
November 10 instead of November 9.

Jews might feel free to treat them inhumanly. Posters and
cartoons showed the Jews as monsters, murderers, and thieves.
Photos were also prepared to show the Jew in an evil light. In
order to produce these photos, two different negatives were com-
bined. They showed the "subhuman" Jews as capitalists planning to dominate the world. How this could be done by
subhumans was not clear, but the Nazis cared nothing for reason
and most of those who came to see their exhibits did not think.
The Nazis also accused the Jews of being the force behind the

Communist movement. All the troubles facing Germany were blamed on Jews and Communists.

There were Germans who understood that the propaganda was a series of lies dreamed up by sick minds. But only a few people realized how dangerous these lies were. The propaganda taught that all the problems in Germany were due to Jews; to eliminate the problems, Germans had only to eliminate the Jews. Thus the way was prepared for the mass murder of the Jewish people.

One person who immediately realized the danger of this kind of Nazi anti-Semitism was Irene Harand, a lovely, dark-haired Christian woman who lived in Vienna. When Hitler's followers first began abusing the Jews in 1933, she wrote a book exposing the evils of anti-Semitism. It was directed to "those in Germany who have not lost every feeling of shame." In September 1933, she began publishing a newspaper called *Gerechtigreit* (Justice). Across the top of the front page was written: "I am fighting anti-Semitism because it defiles our Christianity." The cost of producing this paper was paid by Mrs. Harand herself. When she ran out of money, she pawned all her jewelry in order to be able to go on with the fight.

In 1934, she formed the World Organization Against Racial Hatred and Human Misery, which came to be known as the Harand Movement and at one time boasted 40,000 members.

One of Mrs. Harand's most effective weapons against anti-Semitism was a series of colorful stamps. The first set of stamps was issued in October 1937. Each bore the picture of a famous Jew who had made an outstanding contribution to humanity.

Some of those represented were Paul Ehrlich, the scientist; Heinrich Hertz and Robert Lieben, pioneers in developing wireless telegraphy; Baruch Spinoza, philosopher; Benjamin Disraeli, English Prime Minister. One issue of stamps gave facts regarding Jewish contributions to Germany during World War I. Still another showed a photo of Mrs. Harand herself, who by this time had become a symbol of freedom in the hate-ridden world of Europe. These stamps were pasted on letters right next to the regular postage stamp and widely circulated throughout Europe.

In November 1937 the Nazis gathered together all their anti-Semitic propaganda for an exhibit in Munich, Germany, called "The Eternal Jew." This became a traveling exhibit which was

later shown in other German and Austrian cities. A poster with the exhibit title showed an evil-looking old man with money spilling from one hand and the sign of the Communist party on his arm. Thousands came to view this exhibit. Schoolchildren were brought to the exhibit by their teachers who wanted to make sure they saw it.

The anti-Semites were pleased to see the Jews shown in such a terrible light. But some other people were so disgusted by the exhibit that they wanted to take action against it. But there were few to turn to, and Mrs. Harand was one of the few.

When the Munich exhibition opened, Mrs. Harand immediately issued a new set of stamps with the inscription "The Harand Movement of Vienna Answers the Munich Exhibition 'The Eternal Jew.'"

One night, two sailors who worked on the Danube River knocked on Mrs. Harand's door. "We have come for some stamps," they told her. "That exhibit in Munich is a disgrace to civilized human beings. We felt we had to do something."

She quickly let them in. The three spoke in hurried whispers, for already the Harand Movement had become a threat to the Nazis, and Mrs. Harand was in danger of being arrested. The sailors explained how they planned to use the stamps. "We are going back to Munich tonight. We will paste them on the walls of the exhibition hall. Though they are small, hundreds of people will see them before they are discovered and removed by the authorities."

"Where will you hide them?" she asked. "You will be killed if you are caught."

The younger of the sailors took off his shoe and turned it over. He swung the rubber heel to one side. Inside was a hollow place where the stamps could be hidden. Mrs. Harand immediately took dozens of stamps and made them into tiny bundles. The sailors hid them in their heels and went back into the night. A few days later in Munich, tiny pictures of great Jewish scientists, scholars, and artists appeared next to the posters and pictures of imaginary Jewish villains.

In 1938, when the Nazis took over Austria, Mrs. Harand was seventh on the list of people they planned to execute. Fortunately she was in England on a speaking tour at the time. She never returned to her homeland but continued her battle against the Nazis until the end of the war.

Irene Harand lived in the United States until her death in 1975.

THINGS TO THINK ABOUT

1. First Mrs. Harand wrote a book, then she tried to attack the German lies through a newspaper, but the most effective weapon she tried was the stamp. Why were the stamps so effective when the book and the newspaper failed?

2. Why were the Germans so eager to execute Mrs. Harand? What did they have to fear from the small stamps that Mrs. Harand made? Or was it the ideas behind the stamps that the Germans were so afraid of?

3. From your study so far this year, can you list several different types of heroes? Can you make a list showing examples of each different type from among the people you have studied in this book? Which of these heroes deserve to be on a stamp?

19

Rescue from the Sky

As the Nazis closed in on them, the Jews of Europe looked desperately for help. They looked to their Gentile neighbors. They looked to the resistance fighters of the occupied countries. They looked to the Allies. They found no hands outstretched to help them.

Finally, near the end of the war, more and more of the trapped Jews turned their eyes away from the indifference about them and looked toward the heavens.

And help came to them from the skies. It came in the form of the *tzanchanim*—young Jewish parachutists from the Jewish community of Palestine.

The *tzanchanim* consisted of 32 men and women who volunteered to serve the British by parachuting behind enemy lines, where they were to do their utmost to disable the enemy. They blew up railroad tracks, bridges, and munition plants; they were also eager to establish contact and help the remaining Jewish communities survive and individuals to escape.

The Jews of Palestine were ideal for this kind of mission. Many of them had been born in European countries, knew the land, and spoke European languages as their mother tongues. And they were completely dedicated to the Allied cause.

The job of selecting and training the *tzanchanim* went to Enzo Sereni, an Italian Jew who had emigrated to Eretz Yisrael in 1926, where he had helped build Givat Brenner, today one of the largest kibbutzim in Israel.

Even before Hitler came to power, Enzo recognized the true nature of Nazi anti-Semitism. During a visit to Germany in 1929 as a delegate of the Hechalutz (Pioneer) movement, he warned the Jewish communities that they were sitting on a volcano. Hundreds of Jews were moved by his message and by his enthusiasm for Zionism. Inspired, they emigrated to Palestine. In 1933 he returned to Nazi Germany and then went on to Italy, France, the Netherlands, and Norway to alert and rescue more of his people.

In 1940 he enlisted in the British secret service. At the same time he was a member of the Jewish underground in Palestine. In 1944 he was asked to train the *tzanchanim*. After choosing the team to be trained, Enzo himself enlisted. His best friend asked why he endangered himself, especially since he was by far the oldest in the group. "Voices," he answered, "voices of my brothers crying from death wagons, gas chambers, and mass graves fill my heart."

Headquarters for the parachutists' training program was Cairo. The young men and women had to know by heart the names of the Jewish underground leaders and their identifying features. They had to know how to drive and how to use a wireless. They learned to handle explosives. They memorized a special code, and, of course, they practiced parachuting from airplanes.

Some were sent to Italy and waited there for their assignment. Enzo was with them. While Enzo waited, he received a letter from his small son, Daniel, who wrote: "*Abba*, it is not important if you die. The important thing is to die like a hero." Enzo went to the airport in Bari, Italy, with each group, and as he looked over his *tzanchanim*, he thought, "Eretz Yisrael is not forsaken if she has children such as these."

Wherever they went, the parachutists were treated as heroes. For the poor Jews enclosed in ghettos, hiding in forests, and imprisoned in death camps, it seemed like a miracle that these people had come to help. Free Jews from a free Eretz Yisrael risked their lives to help their brothers in Europe.

Enzo's turn to parachute came on May 15, 1944, but the mission turned into a disaster. The pilot lost his way, and Enzo parachuted into a German camp. He was immediately captured by the Germans and taken to Dachau, a death camp, where he was tortured horribly. But he revealed nothing, and finally the Nazis murdered him.

A description of Chana Senesh from a letter written by a British officer. Five days after this letter was written, Chana Senesh was executed in the Budapest prison yard.

I had the pleasure of meeting a young person from Jerusalem who parachuted to my headquarters in Slovenia and proceeded overland to another part of Europe. She was a grand girl and as plucky as anyone could be. Should you hear of her when she returns, please put yourself out to meet her. She was with two other men from Palestine. They were all excellent and will be regarded as great heroes as time goes on.

Fourteen months after Enzo's death a ship bearing his name docked in Haifa harbor, proudly flying the blue and white Jewish flag. Palestine was still under the rule of Britain, who would not allow Jews to enter the land. But this ship carried a precious cargo that Enzo would have been proud of—a thousand "illegal" refugees, smuggled into the harbor.

Years later, at a memorial meeting for Enzo, one of Israel's leaders said of him, "If Abraham had founded the Jewish nation only for the sake of Enzo Chayim Sereni, it would have been reason enough."

Another parachutist from Palestine who gave her life to the cause was Chana Senesh—pioneer, poet, and parachutist. Chana was born in Budapest into a wealthy and prominent Hungarian

Jewish family which had grown away from Judaism. At seventeen Chana became interested in Zionism. She learned Hebrew and decided to settle in Eretz Yisrael. She was accepted at an agricultural school in Palestine and then applied for a certificate to leave Hungary.

Ten days after her eighteenth birthday, she received the certificate. Three months later, she arrived. First she trained on a farm for her agricultural career. Then she settled on a kibbutz called S'doth Yam, a new, struggling settlement near Caesaria. She hardly missed her easy, luxurious life in Hungary or the elegant parties, beautiful clothes, and fine food. She only missed her mother.

Chana Senesh was a poet. She saw everything—her own life, the sacrifice her mother made in allowing her to leave Hungary, and the country which she adopted as her own—with a poet's sensitivity. Little by little she learned Hebrew well enough to write her poetry in it. One beautiful poem said:

> My God, these should never end:
> the sand and the sea,
> the sound of water,
> the thunder of heaven,
> the prayers of man.

When she was chosen to be a parachutist, she wrote in her diary, "To leave this land and freedom? I would like to fill my lungs with the fresh air of Eretz Yisrael, which I will be able to breathe

THE HOLOCAUST

in the choking atmosphere of Europe, and to give it to those who have been denied the taste of freedom." Then she wrote:

> To die—young—to die—No, I did not wish it.
> I love the warm sun,
> And I did not want destruction, war. . . .

> But if I am commanded to live today
> In a stream of blood; amid terrible havoc,
> I will say, Blessed be the Name for the privilege,
> To live, and when the hour comes to die—
> On your soil, my country, my Homeland.

Together with her companions, she parachuted into Yugoslavia and slowly made her way to the border of Hungary. Meantime Hungary was invaded by the Nazis. But Chana continued her assignment.

After many days of travel through forests and villages, she succeeded in crossing the border but was almost immediately captured by Hungarian police. She was tied and whipped on the palms of her hands and the soles of her feet for hours. The Nazis wanted the secret radio code, but Chana knew its importance and would not reveal it, not even under terrible torture.

Then came the worst punishment of all. The Nazis located her mother and brought her to jail. They told Chana if she did not reveal the code, Mrs. Senesh would be tortured and killed. Still Chana kept the secret. Finally they let her mother go.

162

Joel Nusbacher, also in Chana's group, was captured and imprisoned in the same jail with Chana. He soon discovered she was there, for everyone spoke of her with reverence and love. "Even in the police wagon she raised our spirits as she told of Eretz Yisrael," said one prisoner. Chana was three floors above Joel, in solitary confinement, but Joel cleverly invented a system of "talking" to her with mirrors. Chana also invented a system of "talking." She made large letters from paper, with which she formed words and sentences. From morning till night the prisoners watched Chana's window as she "lectured" to them on Eretz Yisrael and life in the kibbutz.

The guards even supplied her with bits of paper. From these she made small puppets. Then her window became a theater as well as a lecture hall. Finally, after two months, Chana was transferred to a large cell. First she conducted exercises for everyone. Then she led discussions, especially about Eretz Yisrael. She taught two Polish children who had spent most of their lives in prison to read and write and rewarded them for good efforts with paper dolls she herself made.

Chana and Joel were finally transferred to another jail in Budapest. Here Chana was put on trial and pleaded guilty. But at the end of the trial, she accused those in the courtroom, as well as all the Nazis and Hungarians who cooperated with the Nazis, of horrible deeds and murderous acts.

On a gray and rainy day in November 1944, the Hungarian prosecutor entered Chana's cell, number 13. She looked up as he asked, "Chana Senesh, you are condemned to death. Will you plead for mercy?"

"Mercy from you? No, I beg no mercy from the hands of hangmen."

"Then you may write farewell letters, for in an hour you will be shot."

Chana wrote two letters, one to her mother and the other to Joel. To Joel, she wrote, "Continue—never retreat—carry the battle to the day of freedom!"

The hour was up. Chana was led to the courtyard, her hands tied to a pillar. A Nazi tried to put a blindfold on her eyes, but she refused to allow it.

Chana wrote a poem which begins:

> Blessed is the match consumed in kindling a flame.
> Blessed is the heart with strength to stop its beating
> > for honor's sake.

Chana herself was the blessed match who kindled a flame in her people that will remain lighted forever.

THINGS TO THINK ABOUT

1. Really the parachutists' mission was very unsuccessful, yet their heroism has been remembered and commemorated. Is a person a hero only if he or she is successful? Was Chana Senesh a hero? Why? What qualities did she have and what actions did she take which made her a hero whether or not she was successful in her mission?

2. Even though the mission was unsuccessful, many Jews suffering under the Nazi oppression gained hope from the stories of the Jews from Eretz Yisrael who had come to help. Do you think that the parachutists were afraid? What does the word "courage" mean? Can we give courage to others through being courageous ourselves?

3. Enzo Sereni's daughter was once asked, "Why did your father volunteer at his age?" She answered, "How could he look me in the face if he sent others to their death but did not volunteer himself?" Do you think that her statement was right? How would you answer if your father had been Enzo Sereni? If you were Enzo Sereni?

20

Youth Aliyah and Aliyah Bet

In 1932 some German teenagers came to the home of Recha Freier in Berlin. They had been fired from their jobs because they were Jewish. Mrs. Freier became very upset over this incident and tried to help them. But the general Jewish community in Germany felt this anti-Semitism would soon blow over and Adolf Hitler would fade into history.

Mrs. Freier did not feel this way. She was very worried about things that were happening in Germany. She felt one way to help was to pave the way for the boys to go to Palestine and work on a kibbutz. This plan would help both the Jewish youngsters in Germany and the struggling Jewish community in Palestine. Most of the Zionists in Germany laughed at her plan, but a few thought it was a good idea. Mrs. Freier didn't give up and finally, at the beginning of 1933, a committee was formed and a meeting was held. The group was given a name—Aid Committee for Jewish Youth, better known to everyone as Youth Aliyah. *Aliyah* means to "go up" to Israel, or Palestine (as it was called then). In Eretz Yisrael the person who directed the Youth Aliyah organization was Henrietta Szold, and in Germany it was Recha Freier. Youth Aliyah was established January 30, 1933, the exact day that the Nazis took office in Germany. After Mrs. Freier did all she could in Europe, she, too, made *aliyah* to Eretz Yisrael.

Through the efforts of Youth Aliyah, thousands of Jewish youngsters were saved from certain death during the Nazi period. In Israel today "graduates" of Youth Aliyah can be found in important posts all over the country—in the army, on kibbutzim, and in the government. One of these famous young men, who lost his entire family in Europe, was Yossi Stern, the Israeli artist.

Yossi was born in Hungary in 1923, and at the age of ten moved with his family to Budapest, the capital of Hungary. Yossi's family was not much interested in being Jewish. They were Hungarians first and gave their children no Jewish education, nor did they attend synagogue.

Yossi was a boy scout. When he was thirteen, he became the head of his troop. He loved scouting. One day, a letter came from the Hungarian government addressed to the scoutmaster. Yossi read it. It said: "From now on, no Jews are allowed to wear the uniform of the boy scouts or participate in their activities." After

Yossi finished reading the letter out loud, he stepped out of the room, changed his uniform for his street clothing, and left. No one stopped him; no one cared.

Scouting had been very important to him. Losing it left him lonely and unhappy. He turned to some of his Jewish acquaintances. One day one of his Jewish friends said, "Yossi, come join our Zionist youth group."

"What do I know about Zionism or Judaism? I know I was born a Jew, but I don't even know what Jew means. I know that many people hate us and that there are many laws keeping us from doing the things we want to do. But I really don't understand it all."

"We will teach you," answered his friend. He gave Yossi a book, *The Jewish State*, by Theodor Herzl. "You see," said his friend, "Theodor Herzl once knew nothing about Judaism either, and look at what a great Jew he became."

Yossi read the book. Then he read other books that were given to him by Jewish friends. He thought about how he felt when he had read the letter to his scout troop. Though he had believed the other scouts who were not Jewish were his friends, not one word had been said by them in his behalf. Were they really his friends? Or were these Jewish boys his real friends? They were Jews. They were brothers. It sounded odd. My Jewish brothers. But each time he said it, it made more sense. And the books made sense. Theodor Herzl, who had been a Jew like himself, an uninterested Jew, also made sense. "A land of our own where the authorities cannot say, 'Take off your scout uniform, Jew!'" That made sense.

So Yossi gradually became a Zionist. He was the only Zionist

From Come from the Four Winds. *Arye was not unlike other Jewish children whose lives were torn from their everyday world of school and play and changed overnight by the effects of the Holocaust. Thanks to Youth Aliyah, however, Arye was one of the lucky ones who survived.*

Arye's farming experience dates from his Hakhshara (preparation) days on a Youth Aliyah training farm (in Germany) where he had gone early in 1939, at the age of fifteen. His father, a . . . bank official, had been dismissed by his Nazi employer; and Arye had been expelled from the . . . school he had attended. . . . One of his fellow students had been the stepson of Dr. Joseph Goebbels, Hitler's . . . minister of propaganda.

"The farmers around the place couldn't get over seeing Jewish boys actually working on the land," Arye recalled.

in his family. His uncles sarcastically called him "the preacher." They were amused. "Anti-Semitism is a fashion now," they said, "but there will never be real anti-Semitism in Hungary." It seemed the grown-ups knew less about what was happening in Europe than did the young people. Even when Czechoslovakia was taken over by Nazi Germany, they gave a thousand reasons why anti-Semitism would never take root in Hungary.

In spite of his family, Yossi kept on with his Jewish studies. And together with his Jewish friends, he talked about how to escape from Hungary. One day one of his friends called him.

"Yossi, now is your only chance. You know about Aliyah Bet. You know legally we are not permitted into Eretz Yisrael, so we have to enter illegally. Aliyah Bet is the organization helping with this illegal immigration. Now is the time to save our lives. Come with us, Yossi." He continued, "One ship will have 100 places on it. No one, not even your relatives, must know you are leaving. You can't even say goodbye. You must meet us after midnight."

Yossi immediately decided to go. Things in Hungary were getting worse and worse for the Jews. He feared for the lives of his family, but there was no way he could convince them of the danger, so he decided to leave alone. He told no one of his decision. Under the cover of night he slipped out of the house with a tiny bundle. He boarded a boat at the appointed spot after midnight. The boat was going to Rumania and was very crowded. Yossi slept on a ledge on the deck. The motor was beneath him, so even though the weather was quite cold and there was snow all about the deck, the heat of the motor kept him warm. The boat sailed down the Danube, but downstream the Danube River became frozen. They were forced to remain in Galatz, a seaport in Rumania. The passengers were placed on huge rafts caught in the ice and frozen in place. Rumanian Jews supplied them with food and lumber and warm clothing. They built roofs with the lumber for the rafts. They remained in the frozen river for three months. Finally the river began to thaw, and one night they received news that a Turkish coal ship was coming to take them to Palestine.

In the middle of the night, Yossi, along with many others, climbed aboard the small boat and went to the side of the Turkish ship—the *Zacharia*—an Aliyah Bet ship. When it was his turn to climb onto the ship, he became frightened. He glanced down as he put one foot on the crude rope ladder. Beneath him was pitch-black water—above him pitch-black night. He tightly clutched the little bag which he had brought from home. He was frightened. He was afraid he might fall into the water and drown. Should he throw the pack away? Then it would be easier to climb. While these thoughts raced through his mind, he was climbing rung by rung without realizing it. Someone below hissed, "Hurry up, we must be loaded soon. It will be light before we know it." He was close to the top and someone reached out and firmly took hold of his hands and his pack, helping him onto the deck of the ship. Once on board, he found 2,000 people—and coal—and the friend who had helped him aboard, someone with whom Yossi was close all his life. The ship was loaded, and it went out into the open sea through the Bosporus to Turkey. Life on shipboard was interesting. Though it was crowded, it was organized like a miniature Jewish community. The Jews from Vienna even formed a cabaret and added some enjoyment for the people.

As they approached Eretz Yisrael, they were sighted and captured by a British boat. The British, cooperating with the Arabs, tried to prevent Jewish immigration into Palestine. They threatened to send this ship back to Rumania. This time the British put the ship's passengers into a camp in Palestine, a camp surrounded by barbed wire. Yossi was herded with the others into the camp. It was not pleasant, but it was better than being sent back to Europe.

Each one was given special chores. Yossi had always done a little sketching. After his chores he would collect all the odd scraps of paper he could find and with the stump of a pencil do some sketching.

After several months this group of Jews was freed, and Youth Aliyah found Yossi a job picking fruit. From that job he went to building houses. But he always continued sketching. When the leaders of Youth Aliyah saw his artwork, they arranged for him to study at Bezalel, the art school in Jerusalem, on a Youth Aliyah scholarship. He was so talented that he graduated in three years instead of four and won an important art award. He also was hired immediately by the school as an art instructor.

Yossi loved Israel, especially Jerusalem. He said,

There are a thousand faces to this country and a thousand faces of my people. I love Jerusalem's hills. I am not happy when I am in flat country. Jerusalem is so full of history that everything here becomes symbolic. A simple beggar looks like Job from the Bible. Figures in the marketplace look like Kohelet. Nowhere else in the world is the Bible so brought to life as here. One miracle follows another.

He couldn't stop telling about Jerusalem. "Every time I see the Gates (of the Old City) it is a miracle. I don't take this sight for granted. I am still a newcomer after thirty years. Everything is still fresh to me. I have not become used to it. Every day in Jerusalem is a holiday."

Yossi was one of thousands who escaped from Europe with the help of Youth Aliyah. Each one told a different, exciting, and often tragic tale.

THINGS TO THINK ABOUT

1. Even before she began to lead the work of Youth Aliyah in Palestine, Henrietta Szold had already accomplished more than most people accomplish in a lifetime. She was born in Baltimore, the daughter of a rabbi. In 1877, after graduating from high school, she began to teach classes in Americanization to European immigrants to the United States.

   In 1892 she became an editor and secretary for the Jewish Publication Society of America. One of her major accomplishments was the translation of Louis Ginzberg's famous *The Legends of the Jews* from the original German. Her English translation fills six thick volumes and took Henrietta Szold twenty-seven years to complete.

   Of course, she was doing much more during that same time. She first visited Palestine in 1909, and her loyalty to Judaism led her to devote her whole life to the cause of Zionism, the rebuilding of the Jewish state in the Holy Land. She discovered a great need for medical services in Palestine. The country was ravaged by malaria, and there was no medical care for mothers and children. To combat the dreadful lack of sanitation and medical facilities in the Holy Land, in 1912 she founded the American women's organization, Hadassah, of which she was president from 1912 to 1926. Concerned with Jewish youth, she established ties between the Hadassah youth organization, Young Judaea, and the Israeli youth organization Hatzofim.

From 1920 on, Henrietta Szold lived in Eretz Yisrael, directing the work of the medical organization she founded. The small clinics that she and her coworkers established became the great Hadassah hospitals in Jerusalem, among the world's finest medical institutions.

In 1933, as conditions in Germany worsened for the Jews, Henrietta Szold took up leadership in the work of a small organization known as Youth Aliyah. The organization grew as the threats of the Nazis deepened. Until her death in 1945, Henrietta Szold devoted herself to aiding the thousands of children brought to Palestine from Europe, saved from the Holocaust.

Reading the story of one of the youngsters that she helped, Yossi Stern, the Israeli artist, we can see the kind of monument that Henrietta Szold built for herself through her work.

From her life story, what concerns do you think were most important to Henrietta Szold? Which of the organizations she helped to form are still in existence today? Have the ideas and goals of these organizations changed?

2. Look up the word "Zionism" in any encyclopedia. What exactly is a "Zionist"? Why did Yossi Stern finally become a Zionist? Is everyone who lives in the state of Israel a Zionist? Is it possible to be a Zionist without living in Israel? Is it possible to be a Zionist without being Jewish?

21

Hunted and Hunters

Sometimes a murderer is caught by a most peculiar twist of fate—or by a strange set of circumstances—or by a little slip, when he is sure he is safe from harm.

Such a man was Adolf Eichmann. It was he who engineered the murder of the six million Jews. It was to be the "Final Solution" of the Jewish problem, for with the murder of all the Jews—which was what the Nazis hoped to achieve—there would be no more Jewish "problem."

Eichmann was cruel and inhuman, although he appeared to be normal. One example of his cruelty was an occurrence in Prague

---

From The Murderers Among Us *by Simon Wiesenthal. Wiesenthal had
tracked Eichmann for nearly sixteen years without ever seeing him.
The Eichmann trial focused the world's attention on the Holocaust.
Television and news coverage brought the full truth to millions
who had never before heard it.*

I saw Adolf Eichmann for the first time on the opening day
of his trial in the courtroom in Jerusalem. For nearly sixteen
years I had thought of him practically every day and every
night. In my mind I had built up an image of a demon, a su-
perman. Instead I saw a small, plain, shabby fellow in a glass
cell between two Israeli policemen; they looked more colorful and interesting than he did. Everything about Eichmann
seemed drawn with charcoal: his grayish face, his balding
head, his clothes. There was nothing demon-like about him;
he looked like a bookkeeper who is afraid to ask for a raise.
Something seemed completely wrong, and I kept thinking
about it. . . . Suddenly I knew what it was. In my mind I'd
always seen Eichmann, commander of life and death. But
the Eichmann I now saw did not wear the uniform of terror
and murder. Dressed in a cheap dark suit, he seemed a card-
board figure, empty, and two-dimensional.

---

when Eichmann summoned the president of the Jewish community and said to him, "The Jews must go—but fast!" The president replied that Jews had lived in Prague for 1100 years and
were indigenous (native to the country). Eichmann began

screaming, "Indigenous? I'll show you!" The next day, the first shipment of Jews left for a concentration camp, never to return.

After the war, in 1945, when it became known that Eichmann was the main executioner of the Jews, serious attempts were made to find him. First it was thought he had committed suicide. But at the Nuremberg trials, one of the Nazis who took the stand expressed the belief that Eichmann was still alive. The Nazi, Captain Dieter Wisliceny, stated that Eichmann once said, "I shall leap into my grave laughing, because the feeling that I have the deaths of five million people on my conscience will be, for me, a source of extraordinary satisfaction." Eichmann had engineered the murder of 73 percent of the Jewish population of Europe by the time the war was over.

In 1947, Eichmann's wife wanted him declared dead. Once this was done, his name would be taken off the "wanted" list of Nazi criminals. Simon Wiesenthal was a Viennese who survived the camps and hunted down Nazi war criminals. He discovered that the man who had declared Eichmann dead was his brother-in-law and that, in all likelihood, his assertion was a fraud. Eichmann's wife was called into court and severely scolded by the judge, and the case was dismissed. Eichmann continued to be listed as alive.

The facts in the Eichmann case were pieced together slowly and tediously, like the pieces in a jigsaw puzzle. Eichmann was discovered to have been in various places after the war. One of these places was Altaussee in Austria, where his family lived. He fled from Austria and voluntarily hid in an American internment camp. When things got too hot there, he ran away and hid in various places, finally leaving Europe. In most places he hid, he was protected by groups of pro-Nazis and people who knew him when he was important. These men were paid well to protect the Nazi criminals and to sneak them out of Europe. In 1952 it was discovered that Frau Eichmann and her sons had disappeared from Austria.

Simon Wiesenthal could not sleep. When he went to his doctor, the doctor suggested he take up a hobby—stamp collecting, perhaps. Wiesenthal decided to do this. Late in 1953 the Nazi-hunter met an old Austrian baron and was invited to his beautiful home. The baron, who was also a stamp collector, showed Wiesenthal his collection. Over wine they talked and looked at stamps and the baron listened to Wiesenthal tell about the work he was doing. The baron was shocked that some big Nazis were back at important jobs and no one seemed to care. Then he arose, opened a drawer, and mentioned a friend in Argentina, a former German lieutenant-colonel who was known as an anti-Nazi. Because of this he had fled, during the war, to Argentina. "I just received this letter," said the baron. "I had asked the lieutenant-colonel if he met any of our old comrades down there. He wrote back, among other things, 'Imagine whom I recently saw—and even had to talk to twice: *dieses elende schwein*, Eichmann [this awful swine, Eichmann] who killed the Jews. He lives near Buenos Aires and works for a water company.' "

The baron continued, "How do you like that? Some of the worst criminals got away."

Wiesenthal returned to his hotel room. Although he was very excited about his discovery, he realized that as a private investigator his work was done. It would be necessary now for the Israeli government to take over. However, nothing happened because there simply was no money for such an extensive manhunt by the Israeli government.

In 1959 the hunt was picked up again, and it was discovered that Adolf Eichmann was still living on the outskirts of Buenos Aires, working in the Mercedes-Benz factory. He had changed his name to Ricardo Klement.

Three young Israelis took over the detective work now. They rented a room near Eichmann's home where they could keep watch on the Nazi's movements. To be sure that he was the right man, they took photographs of Eichmann with a camera hidden in the lock of a briefcase. They followed him to and from work so that they knew—down to the second —when he got on a bus, when he got off, how long it took him to walk home from the bus, and so forth. They decided that when they captured him, the only way to get Eichmann out of Argentina would be by chartered plane. It was obvious that neither his family nor the authorities in Argentina must know anything about the kidnapping. The date decided upon was May 11, 1959.

On that day the kidnap car stopped by the side of the main

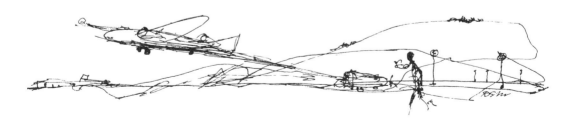

highway which Eichmann had to pass on his way home. One of the Israelis opened the hood of the car as though to fix the engine. The second Israeli was to ask Eichmann a question, and then the two of them would overpower him. That was the plan. But when Eichmann appeared, he thrust his hand into his pocket as though he had a gun. The kidnappers were surprised. One, who was a judo expert, grabbed Eichmann and tumbled with him into a nearby ditch. Eichmann began screaming. But luck was with the Israelis. No one bothered to stop. Eichmann was bundled into the floor of the car, and off they went. The entire kidnapping procedure had taken only 27 seconds. Eichmann was taken to an isolated house which had been selected beforehand. His first words were, "I am Adolf Eichmann, and I know I am in the hands of Israelis."

The fifteen-year hunt was over. But Eichmann was still not out of Argentina. On the evening of departure, Eichmann was given drugged coffee. While he slept, they dressed him and took him to the airplane. He appeared to be an elderly, wealthy, but ill traveler. Everything was done to show that this was, indeed, the case. He was brought to the airport in an elegant limousine with a "chauffeur"—one of the Israelis, of course.

On May 23, 1959, a special meeting of the Israeli parliament, the Knesset, was called. David Ben Gurion, the prime minister, stood up and announced, "A short time ago, an important Nazi war criminal was found. He is under arrest in Israel and will shortly be put on trial. His name is Adolf Eichmann."

After a long trial in Israel, Eichmann was condemned to die and was executed.

Hunted and Hunters

1. The state of Israel has no capital punishment—criminals are not put to death even for the crime of murder. There is one exception: A special law was passed so that Nazi war criminals who had been tried and proved guilty of genocide could be executed for their crimes.

   Even so, when Eichmann was tried and proved guilty, many felt that he should not be put to death. The subject was widely debated. Which side would you have taken? Here is the subject in the form of a debate question:

   RESOLVED: The Nazi war criminal Adolf Eichmann, although tried and proved guilty, should not be executed.

2. Eichmann was very loyal to Hitler. At his trial Eichmann claimed that he was only following orders when he worked on the destruction of the Jews of Europe. Yet the evidence presented by Gideon Hausner, Israel's prosecuting attorney, proved otherwise. In truth, Eichmann often went far beyond the orders of his superiors. Eichmann had become a "fanatic." Look up the word "fanatic" in a dictionary. Can it be good to be a fanatic? When? Are any of the people we have considered in this book fanatics? Which? In what way?

22

A Unique World Court

THE NUREMBERG TRIAL

In the brightly lighted courtroom of the Palace of Justice of Nuremberg, Germany, Lord Justice Geoffrey Lawrence of Great Britain opened the First International Military Tribunal in the fall of 1945. "The trial which is now about to begin is unique in the history of jurisprudence [system of laws] of the world, and it is of supreme importance to millions of people all over the globe."

Four countries participated in this trial: Great Britain, France, the Soviet Union, and the United States. Fifty-two leading judges from these four countries made up the prosecution counsel. (The prosecution is that group which accuses someone of a crime; the defendant is the person or persons being accused of a crime.)

Eight men clothed in judges' robes sat on the high bench of the courtroom. Lord Lawrence represented Great Britain; Francis Biddle, the United States; Henri Donnedieu de Vabres, France; and Major General I. T. Nikitchenko, the Soviet Union. There were also four alternate judges, one from each country. Behind this group hung the flags of their nations.

This international court, the first in history, was trying twenty-one men who had occupied important positions in the government of Nazi Germany. These twenty-one men were being tried as major criminals. The proceedings of this trial lasted 216 days, and 17,000 pages of testimony were written. No trial in all history ever required such long, involved preparations as this International Military Tribunal.

Nuremberg was chosen as the site of the tribunal, partly because this ancient city had once been the setting for enormous Nazi rallies. It seemed fitting that the deeds of the Nazis should be revealed here for all the world to hear.

Since the city was practically in ruins, it had to be rebuilt for the trial; the Grand Hotel and the Guest House, Nuremberg's two leading inns, were among the first buildings to be made livable. The judges, attorneys, and others connected with the trial stayed in them.

The courtroom, too, was remodeled. There were 250 seats for the press, a gallery to accommodate about one hundred visitors, a glass booth for photographers, and on one side of the room, a large screen on which films could be shown. It was used frequently.

From the opening speech presented by Justice Robert H. Jackson, chief of counsel for the United States of America. Although the Nuremberg trials were very important, much of the truth about what happened to the Jews of Europe was not yet fully realized at the time of the trials. Only later as all the evidence was pieced together, did a full picture emerge, a full understanding of the Holocaust.

May it please your Honors, the privilege of opening the first trial in history for crimes against the peace of the world imposes a grave responsibility. The wrongs which we seek to condemn and punish have been so calculated, so malignant and devastating, that civilization cannot tolerate their being ignored because it cannot survive their being repeated.

The trial proceedings were translated simultaneously into English, Russian, French, and German. All the people attending the trial were provided with headsets so they could listen to the proceedings in any of those languages. This was the most carefully recorded trial of all time. Court reporters and stenographers took precise notes, and all proceedings were recorded on tapes and film.

Oddly enough, Germany supplied most of the damning evidence against itself, a complete account of its horrible crimes. Nearly 3,000 tons of documents written by Nazi leaders were found. The Germans kept written records of each tiny detail of their beastly crimes. Even 5,000 German photo negatives were found giving pictorial evidence of the Nazis' actions in ghettoizing the Jews, shipping Jews in cattle cars, crowding Jews into concentration and death camps, gassing Jews to death, burning Jewish bodies, and digging mass graves to hide the remains.

The men on trial were allowed to have their own lawyers. They employed 49: forty of their own and nine appointed by the court.

Since is was a public trial, news coverage was very important. It was believed that not only should the defendants be brought to justice but that people all over the world should know the horror of their crimes so that they would never happen again. The defendants were charged on four counts:

1. A plot to seize power and establish a totalitarian government to rule by force;
2. Crimes against peace;
3. Violation of the laws of war, of international agreements;
4. Crimes against humanity, including use of concentration camps, use of torture, and deliberate murder of civilians.

The Nazis had violated all existing treaties and international law.

Frequently prisoners captured by the Nazis were forced to march until they collapsed. They were stabbed with bayonets, struck with rifle butts, and whipped by sentries. One loaf of bread was distributed to 35 men. American prisoners were starved and beaten. On Christmas 1944 at one concentration camp, prisoners were hanged from a lighted Christmas tree. A doctor testified that he had been forced to remove skin from the dead to be used for lampshades.

A new word was invented—genocide—meaning the systematic killing of an entire nation of people. In Maidanek, one concentration camp, about 1,500,000 persons were killed; in Auschwitz about 4,000,000. In Babi Yar, near Kiev, Russia, almost 34,000 Jews were machine-gunned in two days; over 100,000 people, mostly Jews, were buried there during the Nazi occupation.

In the prisoner's dock, Hermann Goering, Joachim von Ribbentrop, and Rudolf Hess, three of the men on trial, found the proceedings amusing. Their smiles and smirks stopped, though, when a documentary film on Nazi concentration camps as found by American troops was shown: piles of dead . . . the ovens at Buchenwald . . . men in striped prison suits, looking more like skeletons than human beings.

The French prosecution began on January 17:

> France, who was systematically plundered and ruined; France, so many of whose sons were tortured and murdered in the jails of the Gestapo or in their concentration camps . . . asks you above all in the name of the heroic martyrs of the Resistance . . . that justice be done.

On February 8, General Rudenko, of the Soviet Union, began his prosecution:

> When entire regions of flourishing countryside were turned into desert and soil drenched with the blood of

those murdered, it was the work of their hands [the defendants]. . . . In the name of the sacred memory of millions of innocent victims of the fascist terror . . . may justice be done.

The defense of all the Germans was that they knew nothing of what was going on in the concentration camps. All the defendants lied outrageously.

From beginning to end the military trials were the subject of much debate and discussion. Some said it would have been better to shoot the war criminals and have it over with. Some judges questioned the legality of this court—could an international court be a true court of law since there was no world state in existence?

However the Nuremberg Trial marked a milestone in legal history. Lieutenant-Commander Whitney Harris, of the United States counsel, said, "The most significant thing about Nuremberg is that it happened."

Not one person who can read will ever be able to say that these crimes and atrocities have been exaggerated. They are all on the record—for anyone to read.

THINGS TO THINK ABOUT

1. Most of those on trial at Nuremberg claimed that they were only "following orders." Can a person be excused for doing the wrong thing because he is following orders? In training soldiers for an army, countries very often teach their men to obey orders without questioning. Is

this possible? Is it right? When must a soldier think for himself?

2. The trial at Nuremberg was the first of its kind in world history. The Nazis were charged with crimes against humanity. In addition to attempting to destroy the Jewish people, the Nazis had almost totally destroyed the Gypsies, had attempted to murder all who disagreed with them politically, and had destroyed or confiscated personal property and land. But only a few Nazi leaders were actually tried. Many others who were responsible escaped without any punishment whatever. Was Nuremberg a fair trial in your opinion?

3. Germans worked in the offices where orders for the murders of Jews were typed and in the offices of the death camps. Who do you think drove the packed trains carrying Jews to concentration and death camps? How about the German engineers who designed the crematoriums where bodies were burned and gas chambers and the companies that built them? What about the bank in Berlin where money taken from the Jews was put in a special German account? What would you have told your family if you worked at one of these places, or would you have kept silent?

4. It seems as though we now hear the word "genocide" much more often. Can you think of any recent examples of genocide? What are the reasons given for this terrible murder by the leaders who cause it?

Bibliography and Citations

BOOKS

Adon, D. and P.: *Seven Who Fell*, Palestine Pioneer Library.

Atkinson, Linda: *In Kindling Flame: The Story of Hannah Senesh, 1921–1944*, Lothrop, Lee and Shepard, 1985.

Barkai, Meyer, ed.: *The Fighting Ghettos*, J. B. Lippincott, 1962.

Bauer, Yehuda: *Flight and Rescue: Brichah*, Random House, 1970.

Bauminger, A.: *Roll of Honour*, Yad Vashem, 1970.

Berg, Mary: *Warsaw Ghetto*, L. B. Fischer, 1945.

Donat, Alexander: *The Holocaust Kingdom*, Holt, Rinehart and Winston, 1963.

Extermination and Resistance, Ghetto Fighters' House, 1958.

Falstein, Louis, ed.: *Martyrdom of Jewish Physicians in Poland,* Exposition Press, 1963.

Finkelstein, Norman H.: *Remember Not to Forget,* Franklin Watts, 1985.

Flender, Harold: *Rescue in Denmark,* Simon and Schuster, 1963.

Flinker, Moses: *Young Moshe's Diary,* Yad Vashem, 1965.

Frank, Anne: *Anne Frank: The Diary of a Young Girl,* Doubleday, 1967.

Friedlander, Albert H., ed.: *Out of the Whirlwind,* Union of American Hebrew Congregations, 1968.

———: *Leo Baeck, Teacher of Theresienstadt,* Holt, Rinehart and Winston, 1968.

Friedman, Tuviah: *The Hunter,* MacFadden Books, 1961.

Glatstein, Jacob, Israel Knox, and Samuel Margoshes, eds.: *Anthology of Holocaust Literature,* Jewish Publication Society, 1968.

Goldstein, Bernard: *The Stars Bear Witness,* Viking Press, 1949.

Gray, Ronald: *Hitler and the Germans,* Lerner, 1983.

Hausner, Gideon: *Justice in Jerusalem,* Harper and Row, 1968.

Hilberg, Raul: *Destruction of European Jews,* Quadrangle Books, 1961.

———: *Documents of Destruction,* Quadrangle Books, 1971.

I Never Saw Another Butterfly, McGraw-Hill, 1964.

Jewish Resistance During the Holocaust, Yad Vashem, 1968.

Kaplan, Chaim A.: *Scroll of Agony,* The Macmillan Company, 1965.

Katz, Robert: *Death in Rome,* The Macmillan Company, 1967.

———: *Black Sabbath,* The Macmillan Company, 1969.

Katznelson, Y.: *Vittel Diary,* Ghetto Fighters' House.

Kluger, Ruth and Peggy Mann: *The Secret Ship,* Doubleday, 1978.

Kowalski, Isaac: *A Secret Press in Nazi Europe,* Central Guide Publishers, 1969.

Levin, Nora: *The Holocaust,* Thomas Y. Crowell Company, 1968.

The Massacre of European Jewry, World Hashomer Hatzair, 1963.

Meed, Vladka: *On Both Sides of the Wall,* Workmen's Circle and Ghetto Fighters' Kibbutz, 1973.

Meltzer, Milton: *Never to Forget: The Jews of the Holocaust,* Harper and Row, 1976.

Morse, Arthur D.: *While Six Million Died,* Random House, 1968.

Neimark, Anne E.: *One Man's Valor: Leo Baeck and the Holocaust,* Lodestar Books, 1986.

Ringelblum, Emanuel: *Notes from the Warsaw Ghetto,* McGraw-Hill, 1958.

Shabbatai, K.: *As Sheep to the Slaughter?* World Federation of Bergen-Belsen Survivors, 1963.

Shirer, William L.: *The Rise and Fall of Adolf Hitler,* Random House, 1984.

————: *The Rise and Fall of the Third Reich,* Simon and Schuster, 1960.

Silverman, Lena Kuchler: *One Hundred Children,* Doubleday, 1961.

Solomon, Charlotte: *Charlotte: A Diary in Pictures,* Harcourt, Brace and World, 1963.

Stern, Ellen: *Elie Wiesel: Witness for Life,* KTAV, 1982.

Suhl, Yuri: *They Fought Back,* Crown, 1967.

Syrkin, Marie: *Blessed Is the Match,* Alfred A. Knopf, 1947.

Tatelbaum, Itzhak: *Through Our Eyes: Children Witness the Holocaust,* IBT, 1985.

Tenenbaum, J.: *Underground,* Philosophical Library, 1952.

Tushnet, L.: *To Die With Honor,* Citadel Press, 1965.

Trunk, Isaiah: *Judenrat,* The Macmillan Company, 1972.

Unsdorfer, S. B.: *The Yellow Star,* Thomas Yoseloff, 1961.

Yahil, Leni: *The Rescue of Danish Jewry,* Jewish Publication Society, 1969.

Bloom, Sol, "Director of the Lodz Ghetto," in Norman Podhoretz, ed., *The Commentary Reader,* Atheneum, 1966.

Brody, R., "Six Million and Two," *Reconstructionist Magazine.*

Grossman, C., "Revolt in the Ghetto," *Youth and Nation,* March–April 1951.

———, "Mordecai Anilewitz," *Youth and Nation,* April 1951.

Handlin, O., "Jewish Resistance to the Nazis," *American Jewish Historical Quarterly,* January 1969.

"Impact of the Holocaust," *Jewish Digest,* Educational Series.

Jewish Heritage, Entire issue, Spring 1968.

Jewish Heritage, Summer 1965.

Klein, S., "Ghetto of Piotrkow in the Holocaust," *Jerusalem Post,* April 1969.

Knox, Israel, "The Valiant Ones," Workmen's Circle *Call,* March 1968.

Oleiski, J., "The Kovno Ghetto," *ORT Reporter,* March/April, 1971.

Shamir, Y., "Commander of the Ghetto Revolt," *Youth and Nation,* June 1946.

Yad Vashem Studies, 1957–1967.

Yad Vashem Bulletins, 1962–1968.

CITATIONS

The author and publisher would like to acknowledge and indicate the sources of the documents used in *The Holocaust:*

In Chapter 1, Houghton Mifflin Company for Ralph Manheim, tr., Adolf Hitler, *Mein Kampf,* 1943, page 285.

In Chapters 2, 3, and 5, Bantam Books for Susan Sweet, tr., Gerhard Schoenberner, *The Yellow Star,* 1969, pages 20, 148, and 41.

In Chapters 4 and 22, Harper and Row, Harwood L. Childs, tr. and ed., *The Nazi Primer*, 1938, page 13, and Gideon Hausner, *Justice in Jerusalem*, 1968.

In Chapters 6, 7, 11, and 14, *Yad Vashem Studies*, Volumes VI, VII, III, and VII, 1967, 1968, and 1959, pages 132–133, 177 [from Ringelblum's unpublished notes, dated June 1942], 293, and 123.

In Chapters 8 and 10, World Hashomer Hatzair, *The Massacre of European Jewry*, 1963, pages 198–199 and 175 ["Janusz Korczak's Last Walk," by Hanna Morkowicz-Olczakowa].

In Chapters 9 and 13, Central Guide Publishers, E. Zweig, tr., Isaac Kowalski, *A Secret Press in Nazi Europe*, 1969, pages 104–105.

In Chapters 12 and 19, *Yad Vashem Bulletin*, Numbers 22 and 13, May 1968 and October 1963, pages 37 and 69.

In Chapters 15 and 21, McGraw-Hill, Jacob Sloan, ed., Emanuel Ringelblum, *Notes from the Warsaw Ghetto*, 1958, page 154, and Joseph Wechsberg, tr., Simon Wiesenthal, *The Murderers Among Us*, 1967, page 96.

In Chapter 16, Jewish Publication Society, Morris Gradel, tr., Leni Yahil, *The Rescue of Danish Jewry*, 1969, page 229.

In Chapter 17, Ghetto Fighters' House, *Extermination and Resistance*, 1958, page 178.

In Chapter 18, *Statement*, 10 November, 1964. [Kristallnacht occurred in Austria on November 10 instead of November 9.]

In Chapter 20, Herzl Press, Chasya Pincus, *Come from the Four Winds*, 1970, page 50